ACRL PUBLICATIONS IN LIBRARIANSHIP NO. 62

Librarians Serving Diverse Populations:
Challenges and Opportunities

by Lori Mestre

D0556050

Association of College and Research Libraries
A division of the American Library Association
Chicago, 2010

The paper used in this publication meets the minimum requirements of American National Standard for Information Sciences-Permanence of Paper for Printed Library Materials, ANSI Z39.48-1992. ∞

Library of Congress Cataloging-in-Publication Data

Mestre, Lori.
  Librarians serving diverse populations : challenges and opportunities / Lori Mestre.
      p. cm. -- (ACRL publications in librarianship ; no. 62)
  Includes bibliographical references and index.
  ISBN 978-0-8389-8512-0 (pbk. : alk. paper) 1. Multicultural services librarians--Education (Continuing education) 2. Multicultural services librarians--Employment. 3. Libraries and minorities. 4. Libraries and people with disabilities. 5. Library science--Vocational guidance. 6. Multicultural services librarians--Education (Continuing education)--United States. 7. Multicultural services librarians--Employment--United States. 8. Libraries and minorities--United States. 9. Libraries and people with disabilities--United States. 10. Library science--Vocational guidance--United States. 11. Multiculturalism. I. Association of College and Research Libraries. II. Title.
  Z682.4.M85M47 2009
  027.6'3--dc22
                                2009047658

Printed in the United States of America.

14 13 12 11 10   5 4 3 2 1

Table of Contents

Acknowledgements

Special thanks to my husband, Jose, for his unending encouragement and critical eye. I am grateful for the work of Craig Gibson and Kathryn Deiss, from the Association of College and Research Libraries, who helped edit and shepherd through the manuscript. Two graduate students provided incredible assistance: Melanie Marklein for her SPSS manipulation; and Sarah Hjeltness for her sleuthing and compilation skills.

I also wish to acknowledge the Research and Publication Committee of the University of Illinois at Urbana-Champaign Library, who provided support for the completion of this research.

Preface

Providing the optimal library experiences to all constituencies is clearly at the forefront of librarians' service ethics. This includes not only being culturally aware and sensitive to the needs of all users, but also being trained to recognize the various learning and communication styles of others, as well as being able to adjust one's habits based on those differences in order to best interact with cultures other than one's own. In view of the rapidly changing demographics in this country, librarians will increasingly need to work with individuals who have needs and backgrounds that are very different from their own. Yet how do they learn to appreciate and acknowledge these differences, while modifying their own cultural assumptions and expectations to be more sensitive and knowledgeable about other cultures?

Some guiding questions for this study were the following: How do librarians learn to work with diverse cultures; to initiate, coordinate, and expand diversity-related programs at their libraries and institutions; to gain an entrée as liaisons to their various diverse populations? What might be done to better prepare all librarians to be culturally competent?

This book interweaves data from qualitative and quantitative methods (surveys, interviews, and evaluation of documents) to detail the paths, experiences, and factors that contribute to both positive and negative work experiences of librarians who chose a position whose main duty is to coordinate diversity efforts or to work with diverse cultures. The chapters present a snapshot of the training, hiring, support, and work experiences of these librarians. They also offer suggestions for improving curriculum and training at library schools, for seeking a librarian to fill such a position, and for providing follow-up training and support once the librarian is hired. The suggestions can also provide guidance to all librarians who would like to know more about establishing connections with diverse cultures, no matter what position they hold.

Terms Used
Diverse Backgrounds

For the purposes of this book, *diverse backgrounds* refers to the broad range of possible group differences, including race, culture, ethnicity, disability, lifestyle choice, creed, and socioeconomic factors.

Cultural Competency

Cultural competency is a developmental process that evolves over an extended period and refers to an ability to interact effectively with people from different cultures. The National Center for Cultural Competence (2008) lists the following requirements for being culturally competent:

Cultural competence requires that organizations:

- have a defined set of values and principles, and demonstrate behaviors, attitudes, policies and structures that enable them to work effectively cross-culturally.
- have the capacity to (1) value diversity, (2) conduct self-assessment, (3) manage the dynamics of difference, (4) acquire and institutionalize cultural knowledge and (5) adapt to diversity and the cultural contexts of the communities they serve.
- incorporate the above in all aspects of policy making, administration, practice, service delivery and involve systematically consumers, key stakeholders and communities.

The following definition by the Ohio Educator Standards Board (2005) is appropriate to both faculty members and librarians, as it was intended for educators:

> Culturally competent educators see differences among students as assets. They create caring learning communities where individual and cultural heritages, including languages, are expressed and valued. They use knowledge of their students and their families, their communities, and their cultures to design and support instructional strategies that build upon and link home and school experiences. They challenge stereotypes and intolerance. They serve as change agents by thinking and acting critically to address inequities distinguished by (but not limited to) race, language, culture, socioeconomics, family structures, and gender.

Cross et al. (1989) define cultural competency in its broadest sense as the ability to effectively provide services cross-culturally. Becoming culturally competent is a process. Learning how to interact effectively with people of different cultures requires more than just a desire to do so. In order to be aware of other cultures, one must first become aware of one's own cultural worldview and the resultant attitudes toward cultural differences. To move towards a respect for individuals and cultural differences is a goal to achieve and one that can lead to trust when dealing with others.

Others have provided specific goals towards developing this competency. Press and Diggs-Hobson (2005) include specific suggestions for developing mutual understanding with individuals and communities: acknowledge that we do not know as much about other people or communities as they know about themselves, recognize our own and our community's biases, open ourselves up to learn about and from other people and other communities, and work to develop a trusting relationship with individuals and communities. They also provide a suggested code of characteristics of the culturally competent librarians (adapted from the health field) in the areas of attitude, knowledge, and skills.

Elturk (2003, 5–7) also speaks to the need for libraries to become culturally competent and asserts that the services, collections, programs, hiring procedures, and also the physical places in libraries should reflect its inclusive policies and approaches. Two important considerations she notes for being culturally competent are to empower individuals to get involved and to keep the bigger picture in mind. Gomez (2000) also stresses the importance of libraries and librarians being flexible and making exceptions to traditional practice, especially as librarians work with individuals from diverse cultures. He dispels some commonly held views (or myths, as he calls them) about how libraries can achieve cultural competency and provides scenarios of how librarians from the mainstream population (who are English speakers) can become culturally competent in order to be effective communicators, liaisons, and advocates for members of minority cultures. One of the main characteristics he sees as necessary is a true commitment to public service, which means taking time to learn about the individuals with whom one is working, as well as their customs and practices.

Research Design

The study included two survey questionnaires, fifteen follow-up interviews, and scans of all of the ARL library webpages for instances of diversity or multicultural mission statements, diversity committees, and diversity librarians.

Data Collection

Survey 1: Survey to Librarians

An anonymous survey (see appendix A) consisting of fifty-two multiple-choice questions with options to provide open-ended responses related to multicultural training in library school, hiring, and job-related issues, was sent to 123 ARL academic librarians whose job titles indicated that one of their primary responsibilities was to coordinate diversity or multicultural efforts. A follow-up reminder was sent, and 44 respondents (35.7%) completed the questionnaire.

The survey included multiple-choice questions (closed) and open-ended responses that were not drawn from a standardized questionnaire. In the field of library science, many job satisfaction studies use standardized questionnaires (e.g., Lanier et al., 1997; Sierpe, 1999; Landry, 2000; Dilevko & Gottlieb, 2004). Horenstein (1993) and Thornton (2000, 2001) are among researchers who believe that when working with small groups with unique characteristics, standardized questionnaires may not get at the complexities and challenges that are faced by those working in a multicultural environment.

Closed questions may not tap into the wealth of insight that librarians possess about their particular workplace. Therefore, this study also included opportunities for respondents to express their views at length in writing and through interviews.

Selection Process

Although it would have been preferable to include all librarians serving multicultural populations, for logistic reasons this study was restricted to those working in ARL libraries who could be identified as having primary duties related to multicultural or diversity efforts.

The process of identifying librarians in the above category was a challenge. There is no definitive list of librarians with these job titles. If such a position becomes vacant, libraries don't always fill it. In order to get a list of these librarians, an initial scan was conducted of the webpages for ARL libraries. However, it was not always evident if there was a designated librarian for multicultural or diversity efforts. In addition to checking staff directories, department pages, and search engines, efforts were made to consult the "ask a librarian" services to determine whether or not there was an individual who served in that capacity. Other attempts were made by posting to the Diversity-L discussion list, contacting the ethnic caucuses to find names of individuals, and consulting lists of Spectrum Scholar recipients. However, many of the librarians who responded had positions other than those dedicated to multicultural services. The original list was expanded from only those with official titles related to being a diversity librarian to also include those who had some major component of diversity in their job title, such as being a liaison to a cultural group. The final number of ARL librarians contacted was 123. In instances when there was no visible librarian in charge of diversity efforts, a couple of librarians with subject responsibilities to ethnic groups were contacted. Therefore, more than one librarian from an ARL library may have responded. It is unknown if all ARL libraries are represented in this study because it was anonymous. However, a webpage scan was conducted of each of the ARL websites in an attempt to capture the diversity efforts at each ARL.

As a pretest, the questionnaire was submitted for comment to five librarians, two of whom had unsuccessfully interviewed for positions as multicultural librarians and three of whom had positions with those duties. Based on their suggestions, a number of important revisions to question wording and order were made. The categories for the survey were as follows:

- Part I: Library School Information (8 questions)
- Part II: Current Position Information (3 questions)
- Part III: The Hiring Process (12 questions)
- Part IV: Reality of the Job (6 questions)
- Part V: Job Satisfaction (16 questions)
- Part VI: Background Information (7 questions)

These categories will be discussed in detail in the following chapters.

Interviews
Follow-up phone interviews (see appendix C for initial questions) were conducted with 14 of the respondents to the librarian survey who indicated their willingness. Interviews were taped and transcribed using Dragon Speak software.

Survey 2: Survey to Library School Administrators
An anonymous survey (see appendix B) was sent to the 49 accredited library schools in the United States. A follow-up reminder was sent, with

25 respondents, or 51%, completing the questionnaire. There were sixteen questions, including six open-ended questions. Each question offered an "other" or "comments" option to provide opportunity for original responses. A few faculty also sent syllabi corresponding to diversity courses.

Webpage Scan

A scan of all of the ARL library webpages was conducted to determine if the following existed:

- mention of diversity in the library mission and strategic plans
- evidence of diversity committees
- a librarian in charge of diversity or multicultural efforts or a main diversity contact

A graduate student in library and information science also timed how long it took her to find the above using the library's search engine, directories, subject librarian listings, and help and find features.

Content Analysis

Content analysis was conducted to identify themes and issues. Categories and subcategories were created for each question, the results of which are displayed in a series of tables in subsequent chapters in this book. Themes were generated based on the number of times a particular issue or factor was noted by respondents. Because several questions allowed for multiple responses, participants typically cited many factors and issues in their answers. Accordingly, the numbers presented in the tables may not necessarily correspond to the number of respondents, and at times percentages may not add up to 100, simply because one participant could, for example, cite many different challenges at her or his current position.

Demographic Information: Librarian Survey

The first section of the survey asked for information related to age, gender, ethnicity, and current job. Almost half of the participants were aged 45–54 (see figure 1). For many, this was a second position or career. Several librarians had already been in another position at the same institution for several years and moved into this position.

The majority of respondents (89.6%) had been in this position less than 10 years (see figure 2), which seems logical, since most of these positions were newly created in the previous few years. It was a welcome surprise to learn that a few librarians had been in their position for over 10 years.

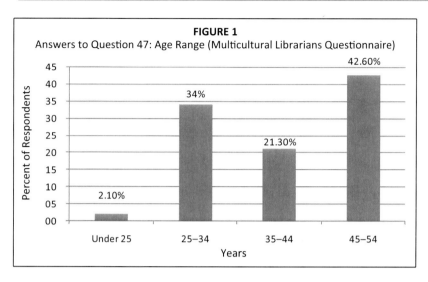

FIGURE 1
Answers to Question 47: Age Range (Multicultural Librarians Questionnaire)

So often after someone leaves such a postion, it is hard to find a replacement, or the job morphs into some other position. It is interesting to note that four librarians had been in their position for more than 15 years, a rare occurrence. Two of these librarians consented to do interviews, and their stories are definitely ones of struggling to find their way since they were pioneers in these efforts, with little academic or on-the-job training in multicultural or diversity issues. However, even the newer librarians recounted similar stories of not knowing how to begin due to lack of knowledge about what someone in this position does, as well as not having had relevant courses in library school.

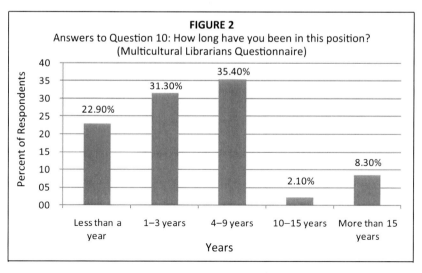

FIGURE 2
Answers to Question 10: How long have you been in this position?
(Multicultural Librarians Questionnaire)

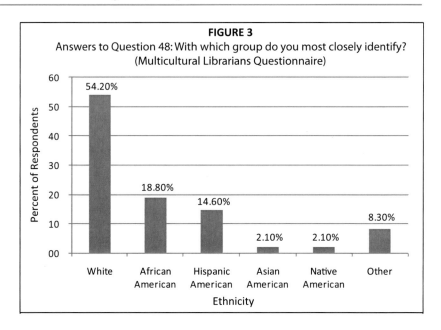

FIGURE 3
Answers to Question 48: With which group do you most closely identify?
(Multicultural Librarians Questionnaire)

Figure 3 details the breakdown of ethnicities. Several librarians chose "other" as a response and indicated their specific ethnicity in the write-in text box. All of these indicated they were biracial.

Out of a total of 44 respondents, 75% were female, which is representative of the breakdown of all credentialed librarians, regardless of race (ALA, 2005).

Current Status of Multicultural Librarianship at ARL Libraries

An examination of all ARL library webpages was conducted to identify libraries that had a designated librarian to guide or coordinate diversity or multicultural efforts. It was possible to find instances of these positions in only 14 of the 107 ARL libraries in the United States. Titles varied and included "diversity librarian," "multicultural librarian," "outreach librarian for multicultural services," "ethnic studies librarian," and similar titles. The majority of ARL libraries (78) have subject specialists for different populations. However, their role is usually limited to specific populations and does not include overseeing diversity initiatives committed to providing instruction, reference, acquisition of appropriate materials, or outreach services for multiple diverse populations, nor does it include training for librarians.

How Librarians Are Currently Providing Services to Diverse Populations

For multiple reasons, it appears that past library efforts to provide diversity training and make liaison efforts to underrepresented groups have decreased in priority in relation to other library goals. Some possible explanations include diminishing budgets, inability to hire a designated individual for such duties, or a decision to spread out the responsibilities among various subject liaisons. This last model is well represented in libraries where many individuals are charged with collection development for specific populations. Although many libraries may have an African American studies librarian, a Latino studies librarian, a Native American studies librarian, or an Asian American studies librarian, most institutions have no single person designated to coordinate diversity efforts. Even if libraries strive to hire a coordinator for multicultural or diversity services, they may find that librarians are not attracted to these specific positions or are not adequately trained for such. Without a librarian dedicated to coordinate programmatic training or to forge critical connections needed on campus and in the community, the library may persist in being perceived as a monocultural, monolingual institution. The need for a restructuring of library school curriculum to provide cultural competency training will be discussed in chapter 8.

Of the librarians selected for this study, 24 chose an "other" category to provide their title. This illustrates part of the difficulty in determining who to contact when one visits a library webpage. Subject librarians were

TABLE 1
Answers to Question 9: What is your current job title?
(Multicultural Librarians Questionnaire)

Job Title	No.	Percent
Diversity Librarian	2	4.4%
Ethnic Studies & Multicultural Librarian	1	2.2%
Multicultural Librarian	1	2.2%
Multicultural Services Librarian	1	2.2%
Outreach Librarian	6	13.3%
Outreach Librarian for Multicultural Services	1	2.2%
Reference Librarian serving diverse culture	9	20.1%
Other	24	53.3%

not targeted for this study, yet many of them also provide such services, perhaps to a focused cultural group. Following are additional job titles that these participants provided:

- Access Services Librarian
- Business Librarian
- Chicana/o Studies Librarian
- Collection Development Librarian and Voices and Choices Center Coordinator
- Immigrant Outreach Specialist
- Latin American Studies and Romance Languages bibliographer
- Latino Services supervisor
- Librarian for U.S. Latino Studies and the Caribbean
- Library Manager, previously Diversity Librarian, same system
- Modern Languages and Cultures Librarian
- Multicultural Services Coordinator
- Outreach Librarian (with a focus on diverse populations)
  —Instruction and Outreach Librarian
  —Outreach/Multicultural Librarian
  —Outreach and Multicultural Librarian/Reference Services
- Programming Officer
- Reference Librarian
- Training Coordinator

If a patron is looking for someone who is responsible for coordinating multicultural efforts, it can be nearly impossible to determine who that individual might be unless the library website provides a page about multicultural or diversity services and lists contact information. Many of the webpages that were scanned for diversity or multicultural services had a lack of programmatic focus or organization. Even if several librarians work together to provide these services, a designated webpage would be easier to find than browsing down a staff roster and guessing based on job title.

Goals of Diversity Education

The goals of diversity education are to enhance awareness of the diversity of characteristics each of us brings to the table and to develop tools for incorporating these diverse characteristics into practical applications to benefit the organization. This "table" is the library's organizational culture with all of the necessary components of a fully developed culture. Therefore, not only is the organization challenged to acknowledge and encourage diverse individual contributions, but it must do this in an established environment that is founded in history and values. To embrace cultural pluralism, an organization must actively challenge the organizational culture and encourage change or expansion of the established culture in order to encompass a broad spectrum of human characteristics and styles.

Cultural pluralism is a confusing concept for organizations and is at the core of society's mixed feelings about "diversity." Cultural pluralism replaces the "melting pot" theory in describing the multicultural character of United States society. Ideally, members of a pluralistic society recognize the contributions of each individual and each group to the common civilization, or macro-culture, and encourage the maintenance and development of different yet compatible lifestyles, languages, and convictions. Equally important is a commitment to deal cooperatively with common concerns. Overall, cultural pluralism strives to create harmony and respect.

Summary

The chapters in this book provide information about the education, training, experiences, and strategies of librarians charged with coordinating diversity efforts:

- Chapter 1 provides a brief overview of the jobs and responsibilities of librarians serving diverse populations and explains the importance of having a commitment to filling such a position. The survey results provide a snapshot of characteristics of current librarians in those positions. Included is a discussion of the importance of training all librarians to work with diverse populations, rather than relying on a single person (e.g., a "diversity librarian" or someone from a culture outside the mainstream population) to serve the needs of the rapidly growing numbers of patrons from diverse backgrounds.
- Chapter 2 discusses prior education and motivation that librarians had for these positions, as well as training they received on the job.
- Analysis of the surveys and information related to the job search experience and expectations on the job are covered in chapter 3. It includes suggestions for search committees on job descriptions, advertising, interviewing, and hiring.
- Chapter 4 presents correlations based on ethnicity of the librarian and responses pertaining to themes. Some of the major

themes discussed are how the librarians gained entrée into their
environments and how they got started in developing liaison
relationships with their constituencies; whether or not duties and
work expectations were realistic; and perceived work satisfaction
using measures related to environment, training, support,
expectations, respect, and isolation.

- Recommendations by librarians surveyed are presented in
chapter 5. These recommendations pertain to ways for librarians
to find a voice and to be recognized and respected for their work.
The chapter also includes suggestions on ways to get connected
to the library and to their constituencies and to overcome
barriers within the library related to achieving goals, including
how to garner support and involvement by other library
personnel.

- Suggestions for organizing and managing multicultural services
are provided in chapter 6.

- The experiences and reflections of librarians pertaining to
working with their library and colleagues to create a more
inclusive work environment are included in chapter 7.

- Chapter 8 discusses the need for revamping the curriculum at
library schools to provide opportunities for all students to receive
a foundational base for learning to be culturally competent.

- Next steps in the development of multicultural services are
discussed in chapter 9. Included are summaries of what
motivates librarians working with multicultural constituencies
and suggests changes in the field that will enhance these
experiences and advance multicultural services in academic
libraries.

- Chapter 10 is devoted to resources that may be useful to
librarians as they work with multicultural populations.

CHAPTER ONE

Who Are Multicultural Librarians?

This chapter discusses some of the reasons libraries should be active in promoting diversity awareness, provides a rationale for hiring an individual to coordinate diversity efforts in libraries, and summarizes characteristics of the librarians who were surveyed.

Diversity awareness, training, and outreach were major initiatives for libraries in the 1990s. Many libraries made a concerted effort to establish diversity mission statements and diversity committees and to designate a librarian to be the point person for diversity initiatives, both internal and external to the library. Unfortunately, initial progress was not maintained, with a noticeable decrease in activity in recent years. Through this study, it is apparent that few academic libraries now have a designated diversity librarian. Additionally, librarians currently in those positions indicated that prior to accepting their positions they had minimal diversity training or library school courses related to diversity.

An examination of all ARL library webpages indicated that 93 of the 107 ARL libraries in the United States do not have a designated librarian to guide or coordinate diversity or multicultural efforts. Only 14 of the libraries had a full-time "diversity librarian," "multicultural librarian," "outreach librarian for multicultural services," "ethnic studies librarian," or librarian with a similar title. The higher education landscape itself is very differentiated: some institutions are very diverse, and others much less so. Some of the responses by librarians reflected a correlation between the diversity efforts of their institution as a whole and library efforts. As previously mentioned, the majority of ARL libraries (78) have subject specialists for different populations. However, their role is usually limited to specific populations and does not include overseeing diversity initiatives committed to providing instruction, reference, acquisition of appropriate materials, or outreach services for multiple diverse populations, nor does it include training for librarians.

Importance of Diversity Awareness

The public is becoming more ethnically and culturally diverse. Library services need to continue augmenting their services, collections, and outreach to better reach and serve these constituencies. Because library staff is seldom as diverse as library users, various cultural norms and expectations could create barriers to understanding and helping others. Becoming more aware of communication preferences and styles can foster a sense of trust and reciprocity, as well as a sense of belonging.

As campus recruitment efforts and programs become more successful, library outreach to an increasingly diverse student body becomes increasingly important. This increasing importance broadly translates into the need to learn multiple ways to facilitate access to library resources. Specifically, libraries need to be actively involved in working with various student organizations and groups from diverse backgrounds to promote library instruction and reference services. Additionally, many undergraduate and graduate students need guidance from librarians to assist them with research and information skill building on topics related to various cultures. Knowledge of diverse cultures also means developing collections, programming, online resources, and communication styles that meet the needs of the broader population. At the basic level, librarians may acknowledge that one size does not fit all and may actively try to be friendly and helpful to all users. However, they may not have the intensive inner knowledge and experience to understand how to modify their approach or how to read cultural cues to effectively work with and advance the knowledge quests of others. They may readily admit that they would like to better understand the users they serve, yet may not go beyond that admission if not prompted or offered concrete training or programs. Becoming culturally competent cannot be achieved with one or two workshops. If librarians are unaware of the impact their communication, both verbal and nonverbal, has on others, they may be contributing to miscommunication, misunderstanding, and missed opportunities.

In order to work with diverse populations, one needs to understand their cultures. Each culture has its own intricacies, nuances, expectations, and practices. These individual cultures may be at odds with the "library culture." Librarians need to find ways to incorporate the diverse characteristics of their users into some practical applications for them and for the library. One area in which libraries and library schools can advance is in recruitment of librarians of color or those from diverse cultures. This important effort can help provide needed guidance and representation. This is definitely an effort that needs continued support and promotion. Chapter 9 will discuss some efforts that are underway to recruit librarians of color.

Value of Librarians of Color

Since the mid-1990s, libraries and library organizations have made great strides in acknowledging the benefits of diversity in their organizations. Programs for recruitment, internships, and scholarships for individuals from different cultures have been very effective. The addition of different perspectives and experiences enhances work in which librarians engage, whether it is developing collections, working with other people, or providing services to a broad constituency. Haro (1981) was one of the pioneers promoting diversity awareness and advocacy in librarianship. He commented that the perception was that "libraries are often perceived as one of many Anglo institutions that are designed and controlled by Anglos to serve Anglos" (p. 241). Nearly thirty years later, that is still the perception of many.

One of the positive efforts now is that libraries are recruiting librarians of color, which is an important goal in helping patrons see in these positions of authority people who look like them and who might have experienced similar issues and challenges. Their input is vital to helping libraries learn how to better communicate and serve others. However, these librarians accept jobs in multiple areas of librarianship, not solely as designated "diversity librarians." Additionally, librarians of color constitute only about 12 to 12.5% of academic and public librarian populations (Saye & Wisser, 2003). The proportion of librarians of color among credentialed librarians has actually dropped from 12% in 1990 to 10% in 2000 (Decision Demographics, 2004). These data are the most current available. As in the library and information science (LIS) student population, the proportion of ethnic minorities in the librarian population (10–12.5%) is significantly lower than the proportion in the United States population, 31.3% (United States Bureau of the Census, 2009). This gap between LIS and U.S. populations may widen unless organizations develop and support a more aggressive recruitment program (Josey, 1993). These statistics indicate that despite all the initiatives undertaken by library schools for promoting cultural diversity, the profession is still far from reaching its goal of proportionate representation.

One of the benefits of having librarians of color working in libraries is to help provide their perspectives on gaps in services and disconnects with communication and interactions. Clearly they cannot be expected to speak for all, yet their voices are needed in addition to voices from the mainstream population. They can also help with connections on campus and with gaining an entrée into different population groups. However, in this study, even librarians of color indicated that their job provided many challenges because they had not had sufficient education or training in library school to understand what it meant to be a diversity or multicultural librarian. They understood the importance of this position and the goal of helping other librarians become culturally competent, but wished they had known more about how to approach the position. Some of them commented that there was an erroneous perception that just because they were from an ethnic minority group, they should automatically understand how to develop programs, provide training, and coordinate these activities.

Need for a Librarian to Coordinate Diversity Efforts

One of the questions in the study was whether there needs to be a designated position to coordinate multicultural services and outreach, or if the responsibilities could be shared by a number of librarians. One respondent remarked, "I do believe that there should have to be a special justification for services to others who form the fabric of the community as much as anybody else. Justifications such as 'assimilation,' 'integration,' and such are not necessary for persons who already live and exist in the community… unless someone else is having a problem seeing them." A female African American librarian shared the following:

> I think that's an important position. I think if nothing else, it's an important position to establish on behalf of the library and the University that there is a commitment and recognition to diversity and multiculturalism and affirmative action. There are students with specific needs. I think that breaking up this position, even in a practical way would not be practical. To say that outreach be given to the person who collects in modern classical language would be really difficult. It's funny because all of us in our own way, and some of us more specifically than others do outreach. We have outreach to high school

students, to education students etc. I don't know how this position was structured or why it was conceived in the way was, but I think that it is an important position to have. I think if nothing else, it shows students that there's a go-to person, which I think is really an important person to have. I think it's nice for the students to know that there's someone besides the subject specialist. The collection will always, in a lot of ways take care of itself. My job is to make sure students feel comfortable.

An African American male librarian remarked:

I think in an academic setting that you probably need a position set aside that is a multicultural librarian or diversity librarian or whatever you want to call it on staff. Because library school and everybody tells you that when you're selecting you're selecting for everybody and you need to be looking for the materials from other cultures and stuff. But the reality is that you have to select for so many other things that the diversity stuff gets the short shrift. The way we're set up, we have the approval process and you go down and look at the approval books But a lot of times unless somebody sets up the profile to include that kind of stuff and the publishers, those books never come into the approval process. So somebody has to be out there looking for them. The other thing that I'm seeing now is that everybody's talking about Web 2.0 and all of the interaction and stuff, but when we start to look at the content and the things they're talking about with Web 2.0, people of color don't even exist. Where are we in Web 2.0? It's important to have a librarian looking for all of that.

I think you don't see the dedicated positions because libraries aren't dedicated to it. They do the lipservice and have other libraries do the heavy lifting. I think you can find people because I've had several library school students come to me and ask me how I got the position.

> There are very few, I think there's one in Wisconsin right?
> and Minnesota. I think that it's more folks not looking
> for those kinds of positions and I think they may not be
> looking in the right places. There are a lot of people in
> public libraries that have more the skills you are looking
> for to do the outreach.

Ethnicity of Respondents

Where are we in terms of providing designated librarians to serve diverse populations? As reflected in figure 3 in the preface, 54.2% of the librarians in diversity positions who responded to the survey were white. Additionally, 75% were female. The ethnicity may be surprising to many, who may expect that a librarian in charge of working with diverse populations would be from an underrepresented group. Although search committees might hope to hire individuals who have experienced some of the same issues that their patrons might be experiencing, the pool of available librarians from diverse cultures is quite small. An ALA report (2007b) indicates that librarians of color constitute about 11% percent of the credentialed librarians for academic, public, and school libraries. Taking into account that in 2002 ethnic minorities constituted only 11.3% of the LIS student population (Saye & Wisser, 2003), it becomes apparent that libraries cannot solely rely on finding someone from an ethnic minority to lead their diversity efforts.

The librarians who chose "other" self-identified as the following:
- Native American and White
- Hispanic American and White (2)
- Black American
- Although not born in this country, so, not sure if just Hispanic is more accurate
- Hispanic American and African American
- Biracial-Eurasian
- People who've lived/worked outside of U.S.
    —Among-southeast Asian
    —Asian and Hispanic

Hiring Solely Librarians of Color for Diversity Positions

Librarians of color might be thought to be the ideal candidates for positions that serve diverse populations. However, these librarians have many other interests in librarianship and pursue other options. Some of the librarians who were interviewed mentioned that relying solely on librarians of color to lead diversity initiatives might also contribute to the feeling of being targeted and may steer individuals away from such positions. Half of the interviewees mentioned that libraries tend to appoint librarians of color already on staff to be the point person for any initiative that has the word *diversity* or *multicultural* in it, which can lead to stress, overload, unrealistic expectations, and burnout. They suggested that other individuals on staff might also be interested and well suited for those committees, exhibits, projects, and liaison work. With training and education, they could be ideal. Simply assuming that someone of color is automatically trained and educated to lead diversity efforts is analogous to assuming that an individual who is tall automatically knows how to play basketball well. Every librarian in the surveys and interviews, regardless of color, mentioned the lack of training and the amount of time and dedication it took to even understand where and how to begin.

While recruiting and hiring librarians and staff from diverse backgrounds is an important goal of all libraries, that should not be the sole approach to a broader need, namely educating all librarians and staff to become aware of effective modes of interacting with different cultures in order to best provide services for them. Libraries have a variety of ways by which they try to address these issues, such as establishing diversity committees and training, but it should be a priority to educate all future librarians, while they are enrolled in library school, to become culturally competent. This effort should not be the responsibility of one person alone, but should be shared by all. In fact, every job description should contain some mention of how this position fits into the diversity mission of the library.

Existing Library Models for Positions Related to Diversity
Designated Position—Primary Responsibility
The term "diversity librarian" may carry many different connotations. At an early stage, libraries recognized that the person in this type of position should not be the only one responsible for training others in diversity or multicultural awareness or in working with diverse populations. However, the roles and responsibilities of the librarians surveyed and interviewed indicate that oftentimes they are expected not only to do everything related to diversity on their campus, but also to provide reference, instruction,

and collection development services to the general population. Many of them felt that the diversity aspect was an add-on to another job. Additionally, the process of obtaining a diversity or multicultural librarian has not always been successful. Failed searches or low numbers of applicants have resulted in some libraries hiring individuals who may not be adequately trained, if indeed they hired anyone.

Other Models

In addition to the small number of designated diversity librarians, other librarians assume duties, services, and outreach efforts to various groups. Below are some of those models.

Position with Dual Responsibilities

These positions may have the diversity librarian performing some other role as well. Duties are often shared in departments such as reference, instruction, collection development, management, and public relations. In cases with dual titles, it is expected that the librarian devote equal time to both jobs. Most librarians surveyed felt that having dual titles made their job even more overwhelming than if the "other" title was incorporated into the diversity job description. Because reference, instruction, public relations, and management were already expected in most jobs, the librarian then could negotiate and prioritize those areas as needed. However, if one of those areas was determined to be equal to the "diversity" aspect of the job, little time was left to meet all of the other goals and objectives of the job.

One Latina interviewee commented on the negative aspect of not making diversity the primary role:

> I think it's kind of detrimental to the position because it can't be just a part time. You're focusing on the outreach and focusing on different groups you don't traditionally see using the library—they're not the traditional students. They don't see the library as a resource the same way others do. From my personal experience, I never used the library, when I was in my undergrad. I just used maybe the public library, but usually my own resources. It can't really be a part time job of "O.K., I'll do x, y, and z and then I'll do some multicultural outreach." You have to keep your eye on it the whole time. For me it

was like "It's great that there's some reference," but the focus was like, wow, they expect me to be out on campus and working with students and making connections and talking to students and that's going to be my primary focus on this position. That's where people might be very interested. But to put it as a side note like, "You're going to be doing all this stuff, but as a side note we want you to do the multicultural outreach type thing." It doesn't value the differences or show that they are committed, but that it's more of an afterthought.

Collection Development Subject Specialists

Collection development subject specialist is the broad term for all of the bibliographers who attend to areas such as Black American studies, Chicano studies, ethnic studies, Asian American studies, Native American studies, disability services, LGBT (lesbian, gay, bisexual, and transgender) studies, and so forth. Many times these subject specialists have many areas and might pick up a cultural area but not have the time to give it the attention it might deserve. It is important to have those areas as a targeted concern, but do these librarians also provide outreach, reference, instruction, and programming to those populations or sensitivity and cultural awareness for librarians about that population? Or are they instead primarily concerned with collection development? If the latter is the case, then this position becomes disjointed. Because subject specialists represent a major path for how librarians connect with diverse cultures, one should wonder about their training in this area. It is hoped that they had some education to learn to assess the literature in the area, including its importance, significance, bias, trends, and authenticity. It would be interesting to get a picture of the extent to which subject librarians do needs assessments to determine the type of material to select. Librarian who select for numerous faculty and in various areas might be more likely to have a complete picture. Because they need to engage with multiple constituencies and populations, cultural competency training should be a requirement.

Add-on

Oftentimes, a subject specialist will suggest or will be asked to add on a population group that had not been previously represented. For example, the librarian for Spanish and Portuguese may be asked to add on the areas of Latin America or Latino studies or support programs for Latinos. This would appear to be a logical choice. However, if the subject specialist already had a full-time job working with the original constituencies, including reference, instruction, webpage development, and collection development, then those efforts will need to be modified drastically to allow for attention to the other areas. Overburdening a subject specialist is a disservice to all populations.

Outreach Librarian

The term "outreach librarian" was used by 15% of the respondents, although it was oftentimes combined with another term. Perhaps libraries perceive this to be more of a neutral and broader title. It avoids the possible negative connotations of "diversity" or "multicultural." Yet, when investigating the populations served by librarians with this title, it was not possible to define it in any coherent way. Some of the positions used this term to be synonymous with public engagement, for working with groups and programs outside of the academic environment (like schools, businesses, health facilities). Other librarians with this title did work with those constituencies but also with the areas on campus that weren't served by the subject specialists. One institution used the title "outreach librarian for multicultural services," another used "outreach multicultural librarian," and another "immigrant outreach specialist," which were much more specific. It will be interesting to see if more academic libraries begin using the term "outreach" instead of "diversity" or "multicultural" librarian.

Hiring Librarians from Diverse Backgrounds

Some libraries are fortunate enough to attract librarians for a position to work with groups of similar backgrounds to their own. These librarians might find that they are asked to attend to all other cultural groups as well, the assumption being that just because they may be from a nonmainstream culture, they will understand all other cultures.

Libraries are attempting to provide the best service to all constituencies with limited budgets and candidates, and they need to make choices. Any of the models above could be effective if each librarian had appropriate cultural competency training and time to commit to the efforts.

Subject Expertise

The subject expertise of the respondents ranged from art history to science. However, the subject expertise of the majority (60%) of the respondents was in the humanities. Table 1.1 details responses to the question about what subject expertise the respondents have. Some of the respondents indicated more than one major area of study, thus the

TABLE 1.1					
Answers to Question 44: What is your main subject expertise (from a bachelor or other degree, such as Psychology, Education, Music, Physics...)? (Multicultural Librarians Questionnaire)					
Humanities	**38 (60%)**	**Social Sciences**	**20 (31%)**	**Physical Sciences**	**5 (7.93%)**
Ethnic Studies	2	Political Science	1	Sciences	2
History	9	Anthropology	2	Geography	3
Kentucky African American History	1	Psychology	2		
Art History	3	Women's Studies	2		
Spanish	4	Sociology	2		
Chicana/o Studies	1	Communication Arts	2		
Latino Studies	1	Education	4		
Hispanic Literature & Linguistics	1	Law, Political Science	1		
Hispanic Studies	1	Business Management	1		
Latin American Studies	2	Economics	1		
Asian American Studies	1	Finance	1		
German	1	Management	1		
English/English Lit	8				
American Lit and Popular Culture	1				
Film Studies	1				
Theatre	1				

discrepancy between the number of respondents and the number of responses.

The information in table 1.1 is also represented in figure 1.1.

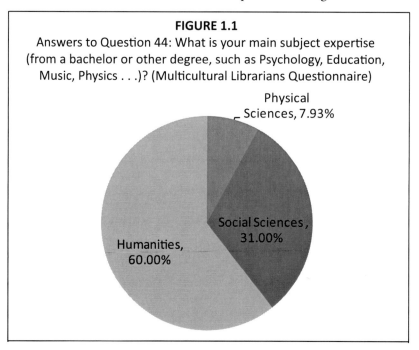

FIGURE 1.1

Answers to Question 44: What is your main subject expertise (from a bachelor or other degree, such as Psychology, Education, Music, Physics . . .)? (Multicultural Librarians Questionnaire)

Physical Sciences, 7.93%

Social Sciences, 31.00%

Humanities, 60.00%

Of those respondents, 29.5% had also studied a field related to diverse populations prior to library school. One would think that this area would have been a specialty of the librarian, much as subject librarians are hired because of a specialty in the area for which they will become responsible. Table 1.2 provides the specific areas of study related to diversity.

Discussion

One of the questions that needs to be addressed related to diversity positions in librarianship is whether or not these positions should be considered another subject-related area. Bibliographers normally possess some strength in the subject discipline to which they are assigned. Many are hired because they have a second master's degree or strength in a given area. Part of the reason for this requirement is so that they will understand the subject area for collection development responsibilities. Another benefit of possessing this subject expertise is that they can consult with faculty and students in the discipline and work with them on their research needs.

TABLE 1.2 Subject Expertise Related to Diversity. From Answers to Question 44: What is your main subject expertise (from a bachelor or other degree, such as Psychology, Education, Music, Physics...)? (Multicultural Librarians Questionnaire)	
Of the respondents, 13 of the 44 (29.5%) had studied:	
Latin American Studies / Latino Studies / Chicano Studies / Hispanic Studies	4
Spanish	3
Ethnic Studies/Anthropology	2
Asian American Studies	1
Women's Studies	1
Hispanic Literature and Linguistics	1
African American History	1

In this study, fewer than 30% of the respondents had a background that included academic study related to diversity. They may have had differing experiences and education, but many did mention that their program of study included ways to identify their own ethnicity and what it means to function both within their communities and within others. Some studied historical and contemporary social events from a multiethnic perspective rather than from an Anglo-American perspective and had training to help them to develop a sensitivity to and understanding of other ethnic cultures and to function effectively within them. Some participants also began developing the ability to make reflective decisions on social issues and to take effective actions to resolve social problems. These are the areas that help one to become culturally competent.

Many other librarians may have backgrounds in ethnic studies and use those skills in some position other than diversity librarian. They may be subject librarians who serve as liaison to the ethnic studies program or to other ethnic, cultural, or diverse populations. If all subject librarians had this type of training, they would be better versed in aligning outreach, collection building, communication styles, and services to match the styles and needs of others. They could help contribute to advancing the diversity initiatives and mission of the library and institution. The diversity or multicultural librarian could then coordinate diversity efforts in a more global way, rather than focusing on isolated sections of the population.

Reasons for Pursuing the Position

Not all of the respondents in this survey intended to pursue a degree as a librarian for multicultural services. They had not taken any courses related to the field prior to obtaining the job, and some applied to the job on a whim. They indicated a lack of preparation, training, and knowledge. Figure 1.2 documents the main reasons they gave for applying for the position.

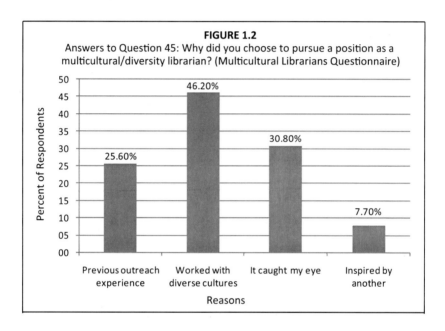

FIGURE 1.2
Answers to Question 45: Why did you choose to pursue a position as a multicultural/diversity librarian? (Multicultural Librarians Questionnaire)

Fewer than half of the respondents pursued the position because they had previously worked with diverse cultures. Almost a third pursued it because "It caught my eye." Some respondents expanded on that answer and indicated that it sounded like fun and it was not something they had seen before. Even though they didn't feel that they had all of the qualifications, they felt that there were enough components in the job that they could do, so they decided to apply. One quarter of the participants had previous outreach experience, so they felt they would be able to apply their knowledge of doing outreach to other constituencies. Others pursued the position because they were already at the institution in some other capacity, one received an internship to pursue multicultural librarianship in academic libraries, and another applied for a reference librarian position and after a few months was asked if she would like to be the multicultural services coordinator. A few had Spanish language ability and felt they could be an asset to at least the Latino population.

One librarian indicated, "I had a belief in social justice and responsibility and a commitment to creating open and diverse libraries." And another said, "We desperately need it in the library and on campus." The librarians who accepted the role of multicultural or diversity librarian did so with the goal of helping the library to be more open and diverse.

Summary

This chapter provided some background demographics on the librarians in this study regarding their ethnicity, their subject expertise, and why they chose a position that serves diverse populations. The data from the librarian survey revealed that a large percentage of the librarians in these positions are from the mainstream population. Due to low numbers of librarians of color, it may become more common for mainstream librarians to take on these types of positions. Because a small percentage of academic libraries have designated individuals to coordinate diversity efforts, a splintered approach is common. However, that approach leaves gaps in the types of services provided, and certain segments of the population may be overlooked. Additionally, if there is not a concerted effort to train all librarians to be culturally competent, libraries will not have progressed much in the near thirty years since Haro (1981) sent out the challenge to move beyond being an Anglo-centric library. The next chapter will provide more detail about the preparation of the librarians in this study.

CHAPTER TWO

Job Preparation for Librarians Working With Diverse Cultures

This chapter presents a discussion about how well prepared the surveyed librarians thought they were for their job. It explores the type of preparation they had in library school and what they encountered once they were hired. An interesting discovery was that many of these librarians had not intended to seek a position related to serving diverse populations and did not feel qualified for the role they undertook. They encountered multiple challenges getting started and provided some suggestions for baseline knowledge they feel librarians should have in order to work effectively with diverse cultures. Some background information regarding job requirements is first presented.

Job Requirements

Several commonalities surfaced from the surveys and interviews regarding job requirements for positions related to coordinating diversity efforts. The first is that the job descriptions, as written, are oftentimes vague, yet too broad and unrealistic in what the incumbent is to accomplish. The second is that even if positions are open to entry-level librarians, there is still an unstated expectation that these librarians will have had some foundational knowledge about coordinating diversity efforts.

The librarians surveyed were not asked to provide copies of their job descriptions or the job ads to which they responded. However, they detailed many of the duties they were to perform, with most including aspects of reference, instruction, collection development, outreach, training, public relations, management, and publishing. Twenty percent of the survey respondents said that the job description indicated that their position was open to entry level-librarians. Reflections from both the surveys and the interviews indicated that the job descriptions and expectations for this type of job were somewhat unrealistic and that often the level of support needed for the duties was not provided. Some of those factors were mentioned as reasons for thinking about leaving this type of position for more traditional positions. In fact, over half (54.2%) of the respondents had been in their current position for three years or less, which would indicate either that there were a lot of new first-time positions being created or that the previous incumbents had left.

Several of the questions in the survey were directed at getting information about preparation and qualifications of the individuals in these positions, as well as reasons for applying for the position. The majority (64%) of the librarians in the survey did not intend to seek a job related to multicultural services, as reflected in figure 2.1, and entered the positions with little preparation.

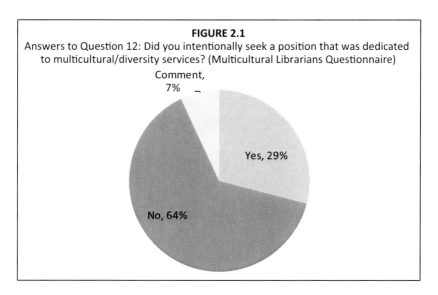

FIGURE 2.1
Answers to Question 12: Did you intentionally seek a position that was dedicated to multicultural/diversity services? (Multicultural Librarians Questionnaire)

Comment, 7%

Yes, 29%

No, 64%

In fact, 34.2% of the librarians surveyed indicated that they took the jobs but did not have all of the stated qualifications. Of those who said they did have the qualifications, only a few were knowledgeable about how to develop programming, training, and campus connections related to their position. They attributed their knowledge and qualifications not to library school training, but to the fact that they had been minority residents or interns at that same institution so that they were familiar with local issues. Further discussion of qualifications will occur in chapter 3.

Library School Preparation
Library School Influence in Seeking Positions to Serve Diverse Populations

Library schools, some more than others, offer courses that could inform students in certain aspects of serving diverse populations. One of the survey questions asked whether the respondent chose the school for its diversity courses. Only two people said yes. One of those stated, "They had an excellent Latin American collection. I was interested in working with the Latin American bibliographer."

Yet in another question, it appeared that others were already interested in the area even if they didn't choose the school for that reason, as shown in table 2.1.

TABLE 2.1 Answers to Question 8: Was there anything in your graduate education at the library school that directed you to pursue a job as multicultural librarian? (Multicultural Librarians Questionnaire)	
Yes, motivating faculty and courses	8.5%
No, already interested in the field	44.7%
No, I hadn't thought of it.	34%

Some individuals mentioned that they had done their practicum with multicultural library collections or had accepted a diversity internship to attend library school, which inspired them to pursue related jobs.

Library School Training

Results from the surveys revealed that diversity training or education was almost nonexistent in both library school curriculum and on-the-job training. Participants said that one of the main challenges they had was not being adequately prepared for the role they were undertaking. Virtually all of the interviewees indicated that they struggled in their position. Table 2.2 represents how well prepared they felt for their job. Preparation could mean either library school training or on-the-job training.

TABLE 2.2 Answers to Question 4: Do you feel that your library school program prepared you for working with multiple cultures? (Multicultural Librarians Questionnaire)	
Yes	21.3%
Somewhat	44.7%
No	27.7%

One of the interviewees provided an elaboration on this point, detailing that his training occurred more from the fellowship he received that specifically focused on training minorities to work with diverse cultures at community colleges: "In my career I guess I was kind of preparing for the position without knowing it. I went to graduate school at Indiana University and I had a fellowship for an institute. We took regular library science classes and then we had classes in the school of education and then we had special seminars to train us to work in community colleges with diverse populations and for the work that what we would do in the community college."

Courses Offered Related to Diversity Training or Awareness

Many library schools in the United States offer courses to assist in the development of cultural awareness, such as courses focusing on various aspects of multicultural librarianship, like collection building for Latinos or specific populations. Many of the courses, however, are geared to the public library in terms of building collections for children's and youth literature. These may be of possible interest to only a small percentage of students. If courses are not required, few choose them, possibly due to the many other degree requirements. Given the quantity of existing

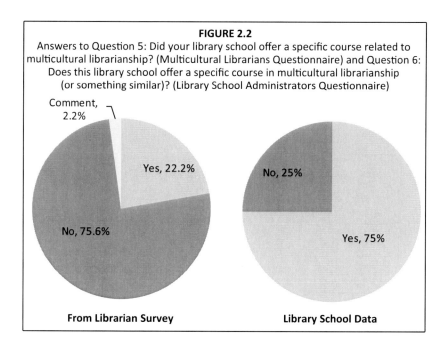

FIGURE 2.2
Answers to Question 5: Did your library school offer a specific course related to multicultural librarianship? (Multicultural Librarians Questionnaire) and Question 6: Does this library school offer a specific course in multicultural librarianship (or something similar)? (Library School Administrators Questionnaire)

Comment, 2.2%

Yes, 22.2%

No, 25%

No, 75.6%

Yes, 75%

From Librarian Survey

Library School Data

core courses, it seems unrealistic to require another core course related to multicultural librarianship, although this would provide at least a minimal foundation for all outgoing librarians.

Even when courses are offered, students may not know about them. Figure 2.2 illustrates the discrepancy between responses from librarians taking the survey in appendix A and library school administrators taking the survey in appendix B, when asked if their library school offered a specific course in multicultural librarianship (or something similar).

Figure 2.2 illustrates that 75.6% of the librarians said a course wasn't offered, whereas 75% of the library school administrators said one was. This discrepancy in responses may indicate a need not only to publicize existing courses more, but to emphasize the importance of librarians taking such courses. The librarians taking the survey were all in roles as multicultural or diversity librarians. Yet three quarters of them were not aware that their library school offered a specific course in multicultural librarianship. Part of this lack of awareness may have been because 64% of the respondents had not intended to look for a job as a multicultural librarian (see figure 2.1), so they may not have looked for courses to prepare them for that role. This speaks volumes about the lack of preparation of librarians to work with other cultures. One would assume that librarians in roles that coordinate diversity awareness and training would have received the necessary training. However, it appears that most of the training happens while on the job.

On-the-Job Training

Beginning any new job requires one to learn new duties, procedures, and skills, as well as to make new contacts. In most jobs, individuals are designated to guide incoming librarians and to help them set up networks, tasks, and training. Additionally, in traditional jobs, several librarians may be doing similar tasks, so the transition may be easier for these types of positions. However, in a position that is unique, without a unit, department, or support structure, the process may become a challenge. When librarians have not had training or coursework to initiate them into this type of work, it can be a daunting task to carve out what should be done. Their support network can be very different from what might be needed by a librarian in a traditional position. Figure 2.3 summarizes respondents' answers to the question "Who did you turn to for guidance on this job?" They could select more than one choice.

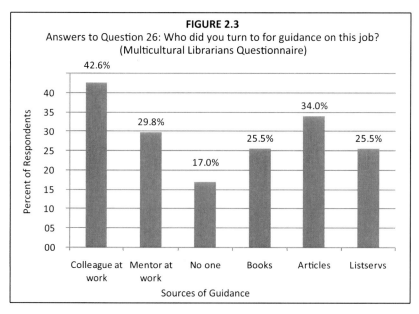

FIGURE 2.3
Answers to Question 26: Who did you turn to for guidance on this job?
(Multicultural Librarians Questionnaire)

An example of the difficulty of finding advice is illustrated by one individual who commented, "No one in the library field seemed to understand." Therefore, she sought anyone she could talk to. Many turned to individuals outside of their library, such as mentors from library school, parents, friends, and people in ethnic studies departments or the community. Several librarians found other contacts in the profession

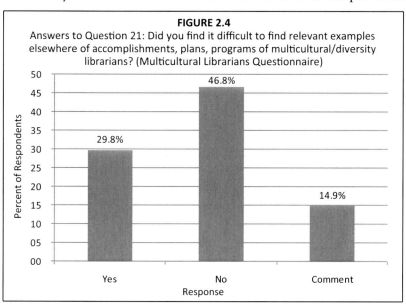

FIGURE 2.4
Answers to Question 21: Did you find it difficult to find relevant examples elsewhere of accomplishments, plans, programs of multicultural/diversity librarians? (Multicultural Librarians Questionnaire)

and professional organizations to consult, such as diversity committees, ethnic caucuses, or colleagues at other institutions. These are all excellent paths to extending our knowledge; however, one would hope that these methods would be in addition to having some guidance provided at one's own library.

Oftentimes librarians enter a job with some framework of what had been done by the previous person or with knowledge of where to look for guidance to help them in their particular subject area. Many of the librarians in this study did not have a previous framework and had difficulty finding relevant examples of what others had done (see figure 2.4).

The comments that were added clarified that many of those who were able to find examples had already been residents at that institution and had been guided by others working there. Some librarians were fortunate enough to not be the first person in that position, so their predecessor might have left some materials and contacts. Others commented that they went to events like diversity conferences, reviewed webpages, or visited other institutions where they spoke with others doing similar work. Several of the librarians said, "I never looked." Part of the difficulty in finding information is that it is very scattered and thus hard to even know what to search for. Various organizations do have nice websites categorized by ethnic group to assist librarians in these efforts. One respondent mentioned

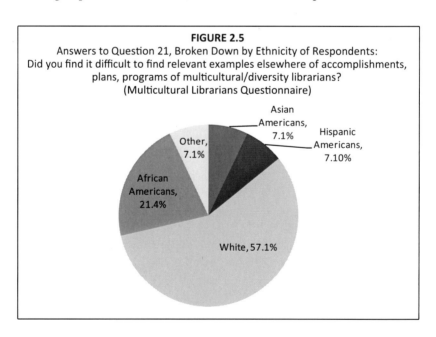

FIGURE 2.5
Answers to Question 21, Broken Down by Ethnicity of Respondents: Did you find it difficult to find relevant examples elsewhere of accomplishments, plans, programs of multicultural/diversity librarians? (Multicultural Librarians Questionnaire)

Asian Americans, 7.1%
Hispanic Americans, 7.10%
Other, 7.1%
African Americans, 21.4%
White, 57.1%

that finding examples is great, but also stated, "Every city and environment is different. Whatever works in Queens will not work across the board. Also, what seems great in Portland, Oregon is not necessarily effective in Indy." Therefore, she emphasized that one needs to really assess the needs of the community you're working in to determine the best resources, programming, and initiatives for that community.

What Knowledge Should Librarians Have?

The librarians in these positions had varying experiences getting established. Many had a steep learning curve, which delayed some of the progress of their work. When asked what they wish they had known about working with diverse populations, including collection development, training, and providing services, these librarians offered the following:

Baseline Knowledge

- Cultural awareness of ethnic groups, including historical, political, and social aspects.
- Cross-cultural communication skills and sensitivity training. Customer service training was also mentioned as being one of the most important aspects of this position.
- Knowledge of major area or ethnic studies collections in the United States. There are various webpages available, but many weren't initially aware of them.
- Knowledge of bibliographic tools (electronic and print). The librarian should be aware of print and electronic tools related to ethnic groups (even how to search other general databases with appropriate subject terms).
- Knowledge of conferences, ethnic caucuses, and book fairs. The librarian should know the organizations and major conferences for area studies or ethnic studies librarians, and the collection development–related committees and subcommittees within each organization. These networking options were very valuable to the librarians, and they indicated the importance of working cooperatively with others.
- Language skills. Librarians recognized the importance of knowing the language of their constituencies but recognized that it would be nearly impossible to know them all. Some made efforts to learn even the basics of the languages. They did feel

that knowing a second language was helpful so that they might be able to understand the difficulty that second language learners have in communicating with others.
- Knowledge of how to set up a training program.
- Ability to lead committees and programming efforts and manage work.

Publishing Trends
- Knowledge of publishers of area or ethnic studies–related materials and publishing trends and reviewing sources. This includes knowledge of the small presses that generally aren't included in approval plans.
- In-depth knowledge of publishing trends, industries, issues, challenges, and so on, both in other countries and in the geographic areas represented within the United States

Summary
While recruiting and hiring librarians and staff from diverse backgrounds is an important goal for libraries, that should not be the sole solution to a broader need, namely educating all librarians and staff to become aware of effective modes of interacting with different cultures in order to best provide services for them. Libraries have a variety of ways they try to address these issues, such as establishing diversity committees and training, but educating all future librarians to become culturally competent while they are enrolled in library school should be a priority.

The interviewees stated they had little prior training for their role, unless they had been a minority resident in the institution or had stepped into a position with someone still in place to provide them some transition. As evidenced in this study, these librarians struggled in getting started in their position. However, a far worse scenario is to reflect upon all the other libraries left without a dedicated multicultural or diversity librarian, whose staff may have had even less preparation or training for diversity awareness, cultural sensitivity, and cultural competency.

A review of the corresponding webpages for the institutions of these "diversity" librarians provides evidence that the librarians have done remarkable work in learning how to create an environment that is welcoming to all, including creating diversity committees, staff diversity training, programming, and developing outreach. However, it can be a daunting task to expect one librarian to be responsible for educating others on diversity efforts.

Becoming culturally competent is a long process. It takes time to reflect, absorb, and then integrate the information. Even if the coordinator provides training opportunities, lack of support from the administration may result in failure to achieve the desired goals. Providing diversity education opportunities for all future librarians is becoming more critical than ever as our society becomes more diverse. If this type of education occurred in library schools, then a diversity librarian could continue with ongoing training and programmatic opportunities.

CHAPTER THREE

Hiring Challenges

This chapter discusses some of the challenges institutions face when attempting to hire librarians for positions to coordinate diversity efforts, as well as perspectives of these librarians of their experiences during the hiring process. Included are reflections about the expectations of the jobs and qualifications requested. Librarians provide suggestions for making the position more realistic.

Selecting, interviewing, and hiring qualified librarians is a time-consuming responsibility. Many individuals, units, and departments (both internal and external to the library) are involved. Search committees in libraries go through an important process to insure that the job advertised accurately represents the role and duties. Writing the job description can be an arduous task. Without guidance from individuals who are in a similar position, it may be difficult to understand if the description and duties are realistic. Search committees do not want to have a failed search, yet anecdotal evidence in the case of hiring diversity or multicultural librarians points to many failed searches.

E-mail correspondence was sent to six institutions that had advertised a position opening in 2007 and 2008 for a diversity or multicultural librarian to inquire about their hiring challenges. All of the respondents said that one of the major challenges was finding enough applicants, even though they had posted to the usual places to attract a large pool of candidates from all backgrounds. All of the respondents indicated that they were surprised that the majority of the applicants were from the mainstream population. They also shared their reservations about hiring many of the applicants who didn't possess the experience or qualifications sought. For a couple of the institutions, this was their second search attempt. Four of the searches were eventually completed. The other two institutions decided not to hire any of the applicants. They indicated that they would probably split up those duties among a few librarians. A survey of their webpages found no indication that anyone was overseeing diversity efforts.

Difficulty in Finding Qualified Applicants
Job Expectations

What should the qualifications be for a position of someone who works with diverse populations or coordinates diversity efforts? Should there be just one individual or several that complement each other's roles in order to provide a team effort? Over and over in interviews, librarians in these positions expressed frustration over what was expected in the job. Two major complaints were that the job description was overwhelming and that the expectations were unclear.

Overcrowded Job Description

Search committees attempt to construct a job description that encompasses all of the duties and expectations that would be ideal for a job. In many traditional positions, crafting job descriptions is pretty straightforward. For example, positions such as reference librarian or cataloger are well established and have evolved as the position has evolved. In the case of a title such as "Librarian for Multicultural Services," the library may hope that many areas will be addressed by the position and include them all in the job description. The primary role may be to lead diversity efforts in outreach, training, and management issues. Equally important to many libraries is that this individual be part of a public service desk, doing collection development, instruction, public relations, committee work, web work, and liaison work. Including all of these components can make a job description overwhelming. At the same time, many of the positions are tenure-track, which means that they also require publishing and presenting. Due to the wide range of responsibilities and goals, one diversity librarian worked with her administration to make the job more manageable by splitting it into three parts. The library now has a multicultural services team that encompasses all of the needed duties.

In addition to including too many duties, many job descriptions ask for qualifications that are possibly unrealistic. Among these are having two languages, two to five years of experience, a second master's degree, demonstrated experience working with diverse populations, and demonstrated leadership skills. Figure 3.1 provides the percentage of surveyed librarians who felt the expectations were realistic. Amounts don't add up to 100% as some individuals chose not to respond to this question.

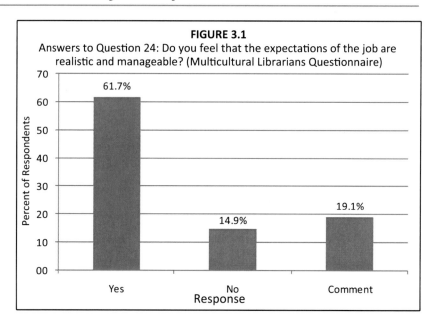

FIGURE 3.1
Answers to Question 24: Do you feel that the expectations of the job are realistic and manageable? (Multicultural Librarians Questionnaire)

For the most part, the librarians felt that the job expectations were realistic, although some mentioned that a couple of people divided the duties or that they had renegotiated the job description to make it more realistic. The librarians who renegotiated their job said that as originally envisioned, the job carried too many responsibilities.

When broken down by ethnicity, the responses revealed that 57.1% of white Anglo Americans felt the expectations were unrealistic, as did 28.7 % of Hispanic Americans. Asian Americans and African Americans thought that expectations were realistic (almost 100%).

The individuals who provided a comment indicated that they would have chosen the answer "No" but wanted to clarify, so they chose the "Comment" option instead. If these respondents (19.10%) had answered no, then that number, combined with the 14.90% who did answer no, then 34% of the respondents would have specified that the job expectations were unrealistic. When responses are correlated with ethnicity, the response is still much higher for white Anglo Americans.

Some of the specific comments that follow indicated that too much was being asked of one person:

- " Outreach is too broad and all-encompassing (always new projects, committees, etc.)."
- "I have another person that is working to cover this issue as well, otherwise it would be unrealistic."

- "The qualifications for these positions vary greatly. Sometimes there are more qualifications than necessary."
- "Depends. For instance, it depends on whether other units are willing to collaborate/support diversity initiatives."
- "The Diversity Librarian position needed more than one person for this area. And needed continued funding."
- "This position goes beyond reference and programming activities. The person in this position needs to constantly search for strategic partnerships within the local community, identify local resources outside of the beaten path and be highly visible—in a way that does not include newspaper articles or TV interviews on English media."

Others commented that the expectations were generally realistic but had qualifiers:

- "Expectations are realistic. Actual workload (outreach coordinator, clerk, page, driver, etc.) is sometimes overwhelming."
- "I chose yes only because the minority student population on campus is still small."
- "Most days, yes. But, there are always the 'out of the blue' or 'knee jerk' requests from above that make absolutely no sense. That too is part of the learning process and educating others ."

Multiple respondents indicated that job expectations were not realistic because there were too many other job responsibilities; it was difficult getting others to work on programs with them; and people didn't understand the need for the position. Another reason given for unrealistic responsibilities was not having adequate support for the position because the need hadn't been adequately communicated to staff, the administration, or even the campus.

Unclear Job Expectations

Some individuals stated that they had expectations of having a clear definition of what duties their positions entailed, yet were disappointed that the search committee itself didn't seem clear on what those duties would be:

- "I don't think at the time I was hired that my organization had really clear expectations. I believe my case was a little unique, as I was charged with outreach to diverse populations, w/ special focus on Spanish-speakers, African Americans, the GLBT community and various other groups. I also chaired the Library's Diversity Committee and participated on its subcommittees as a liaison between them (outreach, programming, collections). The job got bigger and bigger!"

- "From what I gathered from this survey, I am not even sure my job comprehends multicultural services, but again there is no definition of what these are."
- "I found out that because of lack of experience with new populations, the Library did not have clear expectations and their tried-and-true methods were not really effective in attracting new populations to the Library."

One interviewee also discussed the negative impact on the tenure process of having such a broad job description:

> I'm in the tenure track. And what I'm finding is that my job description is so general that it is very difficult to evaluate. I'm in my second year. I'll be asking for specific things that people can look for in my tenure folder. Because I do so many things how do people comment on that? The other issue was that I had to make sure that I was real careful about supervising. Supervision is not something that is highly regarded in terms of tenure. However, I wanted to make sure that when I think of diversity and libraries I wanted to be in the fabric. Before we hired an additional person I was the supervisor, contact person and did instruction and outreach, as much as I possibly could and the day to day stuff. You can drown in that, but I kept my hand in and because I had been on a campus already and I knew the people and departments and contacts.

Suggestions for Setting Reasonable Expectations

Interviewees were asked what they would recommend to help make job expectations clear and reasonable. Some of the responses are detailed below:

- "When expectations are a part of the position description, the funding, and the library commitment, they are realistic and manageable. If the job becomes unmanageable, it should be the result of success in which case there should be justification for more resources in staff, funding, or space."

- "I think that the expectations should be based upon the academic community because if the campus gives very little value to multiculturalism/diversity the expectations of the job can be either realistic and manageable or unrealistic and unmanageable."
- "The job ads, some have too many different types of qualifications or don't seem to fit in with the rest of the library structure, while some are very specific, especially for subject librarians who do collection development and require academic experience or degree."

A Latina librarian who was recruited for her position was fortunate that she had the ability to discuss what she envisioned doing in the job and was able to help craft the job description. Even so, she felt that a critical component of crafting the expectations was the dialog she had with the dean and associate dean of the library regarding her position:

> "It would help to spell out expectations....It's hard to find a direction the library wants to go in. The dean and assoc. dean sat down with us [the other librarians working with diverse populations] and we discussed what we did and what they wanted. That was really important to know the position of the library and what they are supportive to do. That was helpful to sit with them at the beginning and have them say, "These are the things we would want you to do." And they defined what they meant by community and groups they thought we should be affiliated with and to know. Being given the definition written down (outreach to community) is so important. My interpretation of multicultural was a bit different than what the administration thought, like even LGBT, women's group, etc., and when we brainstormed they said, "Oh we hadn't really thought about them. That's great." Defining what they mean and what they talk about regarding the different groups on campus is important.

Level of Experience

As mentioned in the preface, over half (54.2%) of the respondents had been in their current position three years or less (see figure 2 in the preface). This may not be surprising, given that 20% of the positions had been advertised as entry-level positions.

If one were to assess the qualifications for these positions, it might become obvious that entry-level applicants may not have those qualifications unless this was a second career for them. Almost 80% of the positions required at least two years' experience. The expectation of hiring someone with experience for this type of position, along with all of the other requirements, can dramatically reduce the applicant pool.

Desire for the Position

Normally when people apply for a position, they feel that it is a good fit for them and that they have the necessary qualifications. Many librarians aspire to a certain type of position and perhaps train for it, either through coursework or related educational experiences. Multicultural librarianship is rarely discussed as a field in library school, so learning how people came to the position was of interest. Figure 2.1 provides a breakdown of whether or not the librarians surveyed intended to look for a job in multicultural librarianship.

Of interest was that 64% indicated that they hadn't originally intended to seek this type of position. Some of the respondents were already at the library, working as a resident, an intern, or in another position and were asked if they were interested in the job. A few individuals worked for a long time in their library as advocates for creating such a position and then were offered the position. Others applied because it looked interesting, even though they didn't really have training for the position. One individual commented, "I never really thought that there was a position out there like mine. I feel very fortunate to be doing the work I do."

When asked why they pursued this position, survey respondents selected among the choices that: they had previously worked with diverse cultures; that it caught their eye; that they had outreach experience; or that they were inspired by another (see figure 1.2).

Because so many of the librarians surveyed indicated that they had not intended to seek a position dedicated to diversity services, understanding why they did choose the position was of interest. A few provided specific comments about wanting to work with diversity:

- "I wanted to serve a diverse college population."
- "I could be creative and make up the job as I went along; also

had a great desire to make sure EVERYONE got the chance to use the library."
- "My passion at first was Spanish-speaking immigrants."

Others were interested in the job itself, the institution, or the location, as represented in figure 3.2.

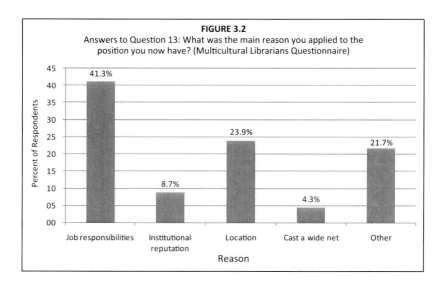

FIGURE 3.2
Answers to Question 13: What was the main reason you applied to the position you now have? (Multicultural Librarians Questionnaire)

In the "other" category, most of the comments were from librarians who had already been at the hiring library in another capacity. These reasons were given by those individuals for applying or accepting the position:
- "A combination of job responsibilities, institutional reputation, and the newly developed department, and location."
- "It was a move up!"
- "An unposted position that was created because of 'restructuring' in the library."
- "Saw deficient services aimed at a fast-growing Spanish-speaking population in Indy. Former person in this position had done an excellent job and I felt there needed to be continuity. I felt I could make an impact by applying my experience and knowledge."
- "I applied and was accepted as an intern by the Dean of University Libraries as I applied to the Library & Information Science program."

- "This position became available in the library where I was already working as an associate, just at the time I finished my MLIS degree."
- "I was placed in this position due to the elimination of my previous department."
- "I did not apply for the position; I defined it and moved into it. We (the library and the campus) needed it!"

Prior Experience

As previously discussed, in a position that coordinates diversity efforts, there isn't always a clear picture of what one might do or what the expectations should be. Until someone is in the position, it may be hard to define the position. In the present study, 40.4% of the librarians responding were the first ones in this position. It may take a new person a couple of years to really assess the situation and determine priorities and needs. To get a better picture of experience required, respondents were asked whether the search committee expected to hire someone who had already established multicultural services elsewhere (see figure 3.3).

It appears that almost half of the positions were willing to accept individuals with little prior experience related to coordinating diversity efforts.

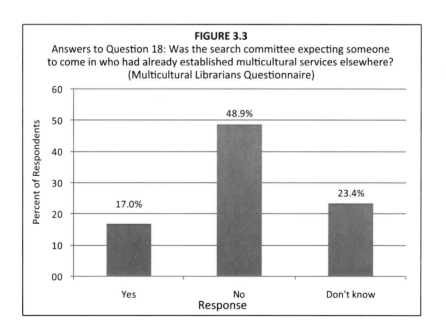

FIGURE 3.3
Answers to Question 18: Was the search committee expecting someone to come in who had already established multicultural services elsewhere? (Multicultural Librarians Questionnaire)

Failed Searches

One of the difficulties that various administrators and librarians mentioned in the surveys was attracting enough qualified librarians for these positions. One respondent who is a diversity librarian shared that he declined a similar position at a different institution for a couple of reasons. One was that the environment did not seem a good fit for him personally, but also the position did not seem to be one with any power behind it. Without some authority and decision-making ability, he was concerned that it would be difficult to advocate or make any advancements. The energy he thought it would take to "persuade individuals" would be too exhausting. Interestingly, the candidate who did take that position quit after two years because she did not feel she had any real support or voice in the administration and got lost in the shuffle. Since then, the job was realigned with reporting lines higher up in the administration, and some of the job duties were taken away to make it more manageable. An African American woman, already at the institution where she eventually moved into the multicultural position, shared experiences her administration went through during the first attempt:

> I was hoping they were hiring someone and they hardly got any applicants. They interviewed the two people and they figured out through the interview process that they weren't really sure who they were looking for and what kind of person who could come in and do what they wanted them to do, in terms of coming up with a template, in terms of dealing with diversity with faculty and staff and collections in outreach services. So after that failed, they came back and they approached me about the position and asked if I'd be interested and what would it take for me to be interested in this position.

Another respondent shared this reason for why he feels some searches fail and why some people leave these positions:

> I think it needs some kind of power. There needs to be a budget and it [the position] needs to have some kind of administrative mandate behind it so that when the person comes in they can present their justification for provid-

ing some unmet service or resource and know that the administration makes diversity a priority. I think it would be an easier fight then. [In my case} the thing is getting frustrating for me. [Because of a lack in this mandate] I got tired and I pretty much didn't do a whole lot for about a year and a half just to kind of recharge my batteries.

These kinds of comments were echoed in several conversations with individuals who felt that the expectations of the job are too broad and extensive and that when they attempt to move forward on some issue they are met with obstacles.

Even if the job description is well written and reflects the job duties accurately, it still may be difficult to attract a large pool of qualified applicants, especially for this specialized job. Some reasons that librarians may not apply to a position could be based on the institution or the geographical region. One respondent said, "Also location is an issue. I've seen jobs that look interesting but, as an ethnic minority, are in places I would never choose to live."

There may be other reasons for not applying to a position that involves working with diverse cultures. Oftentimes the title of a position may carry with it certain assumptions, such as indicating that only a librarian of color or someone from a culture outside of the mainstream would be

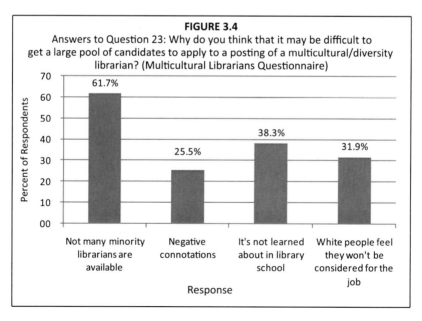

FIGURE 3.4
Answers to Question 23: Why do you think that it may be difficult to get a large pool of candidates to apply to a posting of a multicultural/diversity librarian? (Multicultural Librarians Questionnaire)

considered. Librarians may not fully understand the role of the individual in this position or may not see how their qualifications may fit into this type of position. Figure 3.4 shows the reasons provided by those surveyed that it may be difficult to get a large pool of candidates. Multiple reasons were given by some respondents.

Follow-up comments related to the negative connotations included these:

- "These librarians don't want to be a token minority but would rather work in a traditional position."
- "'Multicultural' and 'diversity' are often stigmatizing terms associated with the 'margins,' marginalized people and people who are other than white. It regularly requires doing the opposite of what is generally done (a non-traditional emphasis). There is too much controversy surrounding attention (often reported as special treatment) given to 'identified' groups."

One of the main reasons suggested by participants that few people might apply for these jobs was that potential applicants lacked an understanding of the position. This comment was similar to comments from librarians in these positions who continually need to explain to others what they do and why the position exists. The whole idea of a multicultural or diversity librarian is rather ambiguous. Many respondents indicated that they didn't feel that people they worked with understood their role. An African American interviewee said, "I think the other part of that is having someone who is innovative enough to take something from scratch and work with it. I mean, I think that's a skill. A person has to have a tough skin because people don't really understand what you do. And because of that, it's hard for a new librarian to be in that because there's so much that's new that it sometimes can be kind of risky, depending on the personality."

Other comments on this topic included these:

- "As I go through this survey, I find less and less clear what is a multicultural/diversity librarian. I don't think this core concept has been well defined."
- "The applicant pool will reflect the care with which the job and description are thought out. My experience tells me that it's not as easy as one would expect to get to details of this sort of job. Most schools go for general & recruit for an outreach librarian. Many interpretations could be applied."
- "It is very rewarding work that can be very demanding of one's

own time. It's not a 9 to 5 job and it requires more support and investment not necessarily tied to the standard measurements. It is not understood what the work entails, and there are always plenty of backseat drivers! There has to be an allowance made for populations with whom these services have not been established versus populations for whom libraries have been part of their lives for generations. Although bits and pieces about multicultural/diversity are brought up in library school, the politics of it all is not explored at all! There are many who are still in the mode of what we think we should provide to them for their 'assimilation' and many others whose perspectives are equally at fault when it comes to assumptions."

- "As an entry level position, it rarely has any supervisory responsibilities and does not allow the librarian to move up as other librarians do. Many white and English speaking librarians give little weight/value to these positions and this feeds the isolation that the multicultural/diversity librarian experiences."
- "Compensation does not reflect the special skill set necessary to be effective in this position."
- "Job stability—lack of postings and many layoffs in the library community nationwide—lack of understanding in library community, what skills the community of color bring to the table—especially foreign born."
- "In the present financial environment, oftentimes vacancies are left vacant or shifting of personnel fills gaps that need to be filled."

Importance of Ethnicity

As previously noted, 54.2% of the librarians in diversity positions who responded to the survey were white. Perhaps search committees may have originally hoped to hire someone qualified who was also from an ethnic group outside the mainstream population. However, for multiple reasons these librarians may decide not to apply or to take the job. Although one would probably not say outright that they are excluding individuals from consideration, the underlying acknowledgement may be that the search committee feels a certain desire to hire individuals who are representative of the cultures they serve. The author has been on a few such search committees, as well as getting anecdotal evidence from other library search committees around the country experiencing the same dilemma. It appears that left with the possibility of a failed search, it may be that search committees decide that the position is such an important one that they may broaden their scope of who to consider or which qualifications are the most important to possess.

These considerations may impact the interview process, especially if the search committee is trying to determine how well someone from the mainstream population will be able to execute the liaison duties and other responsibilities of the job. Some of the responses from those in the position might help future search committees and library administration when they think about similar positions. The first question related to ethnicity preference indicated that 34% of the respondents felt that the search committee was looking to hire someone from a non-Anglo ethnic group (see figure 3.5).

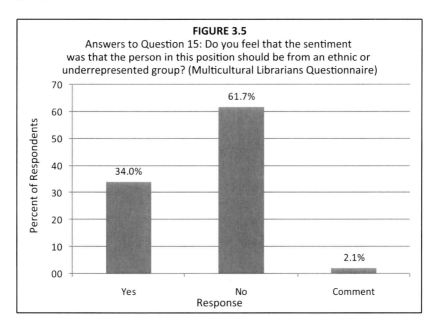

FIGURE 3.5
Answers to Question 15: Do you feel that the sentiment was that the person in this position should be from an ethnic or underrepresented group? (Multicultural Librarians Questionnaire)

With specialized positions, one can include requirements for specific characteristics, such as knowledge of Spanish or demonstrated experience working with ethnic communities. Certain duties or stated qualifications might discourage from applying various individuals who may be qualified, but who don't feel welcome. Of the respondents, 34% felt that there was the hope to hire someone from a non-Anglo ethnic group, even though these respondents were not all from such an ethnic population themselves. No doubt many others did not apply, thinking they would be overlooked.

One of the follow-up comments was from a librarian of color, who answered yes, but added, "The sentiment was a positive one and constructive, rather than forced." In that instance, the search committee prefaced a question with the need to be able to work with people from all different cultures. Yet there were also comments from others who felt some negative feedback from members of a search committee and attributed it to their not being from a targeted group. One librarian said, " I knew that one Latina search committee member from some department on campus was against me from the very beginning and kept asking follow-up questions that really made me feel like I could never do this job because I could not possibly understand how these students have been marginalized or that I couldn't relate to them culturally."

A few other librarians commented that they got the position specifically because they were of a non-Anglo ethnic group and had been recruited, such as: "I became an entry level reference and instruction librarian providing special focus to our ethnic and special communities, such as nontraditional, College Access, and students with disabilities." Another said,

> Well, I started the program and am NOT Latina or from an underrepresented group. I have always tried to hire native speakers on my team or if that wasn't possible, those with the best Spanish and cultural competency. As the city grows and becomes more diverse, it's getting easier to find qualified bilingual/bicultural applicants. We have had very little turnover and a small dept so far (3–4 of us). If I were to leave my position, it would be ideal to hire a bilingual/bicultural person for it if that person also had the necessary skills to perform all the duties.

In many cases the pool of applicants was so small that adjustments had to be made. One person mentioned, "The administration originally wanted to hire a Spanish-speaking librarian. I agreed to learn Spanish while working." Another said, "There were very few applicants that qualified on the job merits, so I think they would have hired anyone with the right academic and library background."

Most of the librarians (70.2%) did not feel that it was necessary to hire someone from outside of the mainstream population. This is encouraging as libraries attempt to create or fill these positions. However, many respondents cued in on the word "necessary" in the question and qualified their answers.

Ethnicity Is Important

The following comments may suggest that, although perhaps not crucial, many believe that coming from a minority culture may prove advantageous for the library's ability to perform these duties.

- "No, it is not 'necessary' to be a minority, but it is helpful in terms of background experience, etc."
- "Ethnic and cultural identity provide much needed understanding of behaviors that affect learning."
- "I said no, but the answer to your question would be different in a more diverse community—it would be more important to be outside the dominant culture in that case, but not necessary."
- "I don't believe that it is necessary, however, I do think that a minority person in the position would be somewhat more well received."
- "I believe it requires someone who is comfortable with and clear about his/her own identity."
- "Not necessarily, but members of ethnic and cultural groups appreciate having someone of color in this position."
- "They have the capabilities to understand underrepresented groups"
- "New American communities, particularly Spanish-speaking ones, tend to be very insular and whatever marketing and outreach methods work for the general population does not work in these communities."
- "Absolutely preferred, but not necessary, and obviously not the only requirement."

Ethnicity Is Not Critical (but with Certain Conditions)

Other comments indicated that some participants felt that ethnicity was not critical to performing the job, but they often qualified their responses:

- "If the person from the dominant culture is working with various cultures and has an understanding of the disparities in society, then they can do a good job. They will also have an understanding of the disadvantages of having a person of color in the position and seek out other persons of color to consider the library profession."

- "Since the position also involves collection development and reference work, academic background and library skills play an important role."
- "It is required for my position to be fluent in Spanish, though I can get by not being a native speaker since others on my team do the translating work in the department."
- "There is always an advantage to having an inclusive staff—but it is not a requirement—I have not felt at a loss work effectively with the wider community because I am Anglo."
- "While that would probably be helpful, and while I do worry sometimes about being a white woman in this position, I think it is far more important to hire someone who understands the value of the work and who is willing to learn."
- "It's hard to know the expectations of each culture. That's what I learned with the international students. It's sometimes challenging culturally. Although I'm Latina and might know if something won't fly with folks in my culture, I don't have a lot of experience with any of the Asian or Middle Eastern students. So you have to learn the social norms of each group."
- "Unless you're able to connect to different cultures you may not know that what's good and works for one culture may not work for others."

One interviewee had helped in the interview process of another librarian to serve as multicultural librarian. She shared that they were intentionally looking for someone outside of the mainstream population, but indicated that those from the mainstream who applied were also good applicants. In response to the question "How do we get librarians coming out into the field or in the field to really think this might be an interesting position?" she said:

> Oh, that's a good question. I think people who are inter-
> viewing for this position should ask that question. And there
> are people from the mainstream who are interested because
> of their past experiences working with diverse people or
> they really knew they had something to contribute to the

program. And so it was really interesting to see the pool this last search. We had a really good pool. But we did feel that the people we interviewed could have done the job even though their experiences were from the mainstream. I think of course if we're trying to increase the diverse people on our staff that means it was a slight drawback for them. But they definitely have the resources to be able to do the job. I think their outreach and ability to reach out and build networks and bridges would've been fine.

The next survey question asked about the role of the candidate's ethnicity in the interview process to determine if they felt it had an impact or not (figure 3.6).

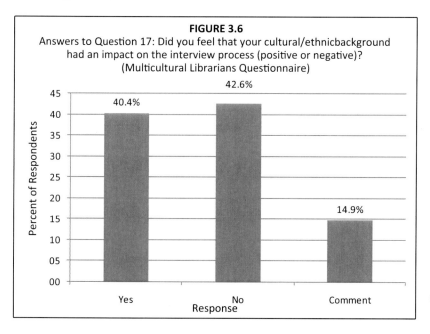

FIGURE 3.6
Answers to Question 17: Did you feel that your cultural/ethnicbackground had an impact on the interview process (positive or negative)? (Multicultural Librarians Questionnaire)

This is a very subjective question and not one that could necessarily be answered with much evidence. Many felt the need to provide additional comments related to this question, with many sharing examples of the value they provided based on their own education in diversity matters and their desire to work with other communities.

One individual related the question of background to religion, indicating how it's really the desire of an individual to forge ahead that can make an impact, regardless of background. She said, "I'm Jewish working in a Catholic institution. When I was hired we had a diversity grant so my hire could have been justified that way. I was told that I was by far the most qualified, and my job doesn't focus on diversity issues. It was my idea to get involved in multicultural issues, based on student population and their needs, not on my job title or any administrative directive." Another individual had already been employed at the library and involved in diversity matters, and although she is African American, she felt that it was what she had done that really made the difference: "Not my background, but self-educating myself in matters of diversity and participation on the Library's Diversity Committee." Another said, "I think that my range of skills and my passion for serving the community had an impact."

Several librarians acknowledged that they felt their ethnicity was considered during the job interview.

- "My appointment to a rather undefined position was without an interview process and I believe my cultural/ethnic background and my life experience has helped make the position grow in credibility."
- "Yes, this was a second career for me and I had lived in several states and being a southerner gave me experiences for dealing with intolerance and insensitivity to discrimination of people of color. Since the Dean at the time was a southerner, we could connect on wanting to move beyond the Civil Rights Movement, especially since we were now in the Midwest."
- "Even though there were no obvious signs, I felt I had to walk a very thin line to avoid letting my ethnic background weigh negatively during my interview."

Qualifications

As mentioned in previous chapters, the librarians surveyed indicated that they did not feel as though they had adequate training for this type of position. Yet many still applied. As stated in chapter 2, over one third (34.2%) of the respondents indicated that they did not feel they had all of the needed qualifications. Of interest is how the statistics break down by ethnicity to this question. Of the participants who said they were qualified, 60% were white, 16.7% were Hispanics, 10% were African Americans, and 3.3% were Asian American. It's unclear if those responses focused on qualifications as written in the job description or a general sense of feeling qualified.

Even for those who said they did have the qualifications, only a few were knowledgeable about how to develop programming, training, and campus connections related to their position. Librarians who provided comments indicated that they had some of the qualifications and felt that the search committee understood they would need some on-the-job training. Some of the comments indicated that they were uncertain since the expectations of the job were not very clearly defined:

- "I really was not sure since it hadn't been done before. I have been able to make my strong attributes work for this position, but I do wonder if the position had been advertised originally if I would have met all the qualifications."
- "I'm not saying I was the most qualified person in the country for the job, but possibly here; and I was in the right place at the right time. I was the very first Spanish speaker at our library (started 9 years ago), and broke new ground at the time creating the program, so it was sort of a learning process. There wasn't a lot of other things to compare to in our area so I didn't feel under qualified."
- "I think definitely maturity is important, especially if the institution doesn't really know what they want in the position. And I think the other part of that is having someone who is innovative enough to take something from scratch and work with it. I think that's a skill that a person has to have and to have a tough skin because people don't really understand what you do. And because of that, it's hard for a new librarian to be in that because there's so much that's new that it sometimes can be kind of risky depending on the personality."
- "There was a level of know how [knowledge] I was going to acquire, but the core of the work was based on my experience and skill in these services."
- "I think I had some qualifications/skills but not all."
- "Qualifications, skills, and experiences for the position went formally unexpressed. Still, it seemed there was confidence that I could do the job."
- "I came to this job with some prior experience working in a library and the skills I had acquired as a teacher and procedure writer gave me confidence that I only needed to focus more on my technology skills."

- "The only qualification I lacked was MLS; however, I was hired with the promise this library would pay for me to obtain MLS. This requirement was dropped when the Library decided to cancel Library School reimbursements."
- "The position is still being developed and the expectations change with the goals of the library and the university."

Even though many of the librarians did not feel they had all of the requested qualifications, they did feel they had considerable attributes that were important for the job. Those are reflected in figure 3.7.

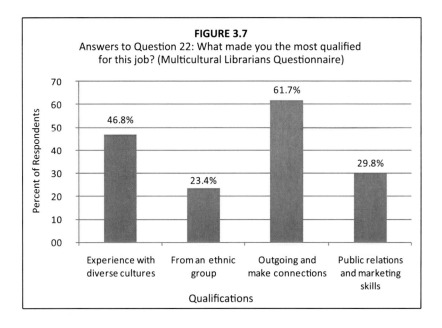

FIGURE 3.7
Answers to Question 22: What made you the most qualified for this job? (Multicultural Librarians Questionnaire)

Many of the librarians felt that their subject expertise was the deciding factor. Others commented about the importance in this type of position of being outgoing and making external connections, regardless of one's ethnicity.

Suggestions for Improving the Search Experience
Search Process

Most librarians in the study said that they never knew there was such a position until they happened to see some jobs posted. Even so, they were unsure what a position like this would entail so were reluctant to apply. Once they spoke with people, it helped alleviate some of the uncertainty about the duties of the position. To help facilitate that process, a goal could be for library search committees to have the search process ready by the ALA Midwinter Meeting so that representatives can go to the ALA job fair to speak with candidates and also to distribute job announcements during the various ethnic caucuses, committees, and programs.

Another great recruiting technique is to rely on the networking that is done at these conferences. Librarians, directors, and associate directors can talk to individuals. A very effective strategy is keeping a position like this in mind anytime one has an opportunity to speak with librarians. One librarian (a Latina) had no intention of leaving her position, but was at a dinner at a conference with some other librarians and that conversation and connection inspired her to pursue the position: "I went to ACRL and met people from a library who, in a conversation over dinner were talking about things I'd be interested doing in a position….It was just a dinner conversation and they asked what kind of jobs I'd like and they said, 'Let me tell you about this position that we have at our university,' and they talked about the things the position would do….After ACRL they started writing me about the position and to apply."

For a position such as this one, getting out to talk with people may be the best recruiting tool, rather than waiting and hoping for the "right" individuals to apply to the position. Many folks may overlook the job description, perhaps not fully understanding what the job entails or how they would fit into that role. Developing a personal connection and rapport with possible candidates may help them visualize the possibilities and then consider the position. Any librarian attending conferences or committee meetings could serve a recruitment role.

Job Descriptions for Diversity Librarians

Many job descriptions and announcements are unappealing and lack creativity (Adcock et al., n.d.). The authors recommended reworking the description to make it more attractive to a greater pool of applicants. If the job is in a different geographic location (and especially a different cultural community), it is important to entice possible applicants with the positives not only of the library and campus, but also of the area. Especially important is to indicate how the library and university value diversity with examples of programs, initiatives, and community building being done. Many of the librarians surveyed mentioned that it was important to also indicate potential for career advancement. They wanted to know that this job was one that could evolve or that they might have the potential for upward movement.

Some questions one might answer when designing the job description are:

- Is the position description written in a way that would welcome those from diverse backgrounds?
- What can be done to increase minority applicants in the pool?
- Does the workplace climate support diversity? If not, what measures are going to be undertaken to address it?
- Is there staff development training that will educate staff members to the importance of having a diverse work force?
- When people of color are in place and excel in their jobs, are there plans and mechanisms to promote them?
- Is there a mentoring program for people of color?

All of these issues need to be addressed when trying to achieve a diverse workplace.

Individuals from various ethnic groups could also be consulted for feedback on job descriptions prior to posting them. They may be able to offer advice on how to make it more enticing to individuals from that cultural group. Most institutions automatically distribute job announcements to minority associations like BCALA, CALA, and REFORMA* as well as their newsletters and electronic discussion lists. Other considerations would be to send them to the residents, fellows, and Spectrum Scholars, past and present.

Summary

Librarians applying to these positions and members of search committees indicated difficulties and challenges in the hiring process. The librarians felt that the job descriptions were very vague, yet overwhelming, and perhaps unrealistic in what needed to be covered. Search committee members found low numbers of applicants and then were concerned about the qualifications. Many of the librarians hired walked into newly created positions and encountered many challenges even understanding what was expected. They also confronted some work satisfaction issues. In order to

*BCALA is the Black Caucus of the American Library Association. CALA is the Chinese American Librarians Association. REFORMA is the National Association to Promote Library & Information Science to Latinos and the Spanish Speaking.

increase efforts to attract librarians to these designated positions, library administration may need to rethink the focus of these positions and be prepared to support and advocate for these positions. Clearly, much more needs to be done to educate the library world about the value of these positions and also to increase their visibility so that other librarians may be motivated to apply.

CHAPTER FOUR

The Realities of This Position

Positions that require librarians to forge relationships with populations that have previously been underserved require the ability to negotiate entrées, to build connections, and to develop rapport with constituencies that may have different communication and interaction expectations. Oftentimes, a librarian for multicultural services is also expected to assist the staff and administration in developing cultural competency. These endeavors involve skills that are not taught formally in library school and are usually in addition to reference, instruction, collection development, and Web development. Adding to the challenge is that of starting a new program from scratch.

One of the rewarding aspects of developing a position is the flexibility allowed in determining priorities and initial efforts. However, this same flexibility can result in frustration if there is not sufficient support from the library administration or acknowledgement of those efforts. Additionally, having too many other responsibilities may mean that certain goals get pushed to the bottom of the list of priorities. This chapter provides reflections and responses from librarians regarding the realities of the position.

Job Satisfaction

Chapter 3 included remarks by librarians surveyed concerning how overwhelming their job can be due to unrealistic expectations placed on them and the difficulty in accomplishing those expectations without adequate library administrative support. Further probing provided additional issues related to the job. These librarians faced various challenges. Figure 4.1 provides a breakdown of some of the most challenging.

Librarians reported different challenges, depending upon their experiences, environment, and support. Some chose to write a comment instead of selecting a response. Figure 4.1 shows that there appears to be no one challenge cited more than any other, and that they are all pretty equal. However, when correlated with ethnicity, various challenges become much

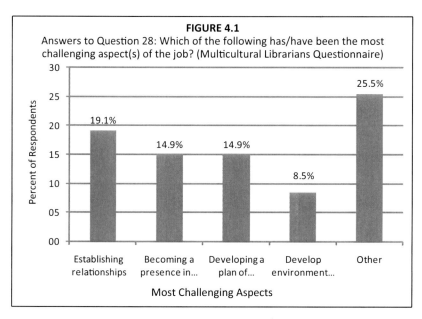

FIGURE 4.1
Answers to Question 28: Which of the following has/have been the most challenging aspect(s) of the job? (Multicultural Librarians Questionnaire)

more predominant, especially for white Anglo Americans and Hispanic Americans. These challenges may say a bit about the comfort level of working with diverse cultures. For example, white Anglo Americans were most concerned with establishing relationships, and Hispanic Americans were most concerned with developing an environment that embraces diversity (see table 4.1)

Several of the respondents chose "other" in response to this question and then combined several of the choices, indicating that they could not choose just one major challenge. Developing a plan of action AND de-

TABLE 4.1
Answers to Question 28, Broken Down by Ethnicity of Respondents: Which of the following has/have been the most challenging aspect(s) of the job? (Multicultural Librarians Questionnaire)

Challenge	Ethnicity	Percentage Selecting
Establishing relationships	White, Anglo Americans	66.7%
	Asian Americans	32%
Becoming a presence	African Americans	28.6%
Developing a plan of action	Other (biracial)	28.6%
Developing an environment that embraces diversity	Hispanic Americans	50%

veloping an environment that embraces diversity were the most common areas joined together. Most of the "other" comments can be divided into two themes: balancing responsibilities and budget concerns.

Balancing Responsibilities

The theme of balancing responsibilities pertains to the difficulty in getting everything done. The following comments illustrate this point:

- "Job was great but a tad stressful—I was always multi-tasking; working with many different kinds of people; training staff (some not receptive!); lots of politics—inside and outside of my library system; lots of irregular hours so I could meet with various outside groups during the times they met; etc. Too little money for the work."
- "Keeping a hand in all of the above. The dynamic nature of academic environments requires action on multiple fronts such as curriculum development, assessment, faculty development, student recruitment and orientation, and information competency."
- "Time. Time. Time!!! It's a huge organization and there's only me to do this work and there really is too much to do."
- "We have a strong tradition of outreach to the immigrant community and now expanding to 'first generation library users' and so getting buy in and support in the institution has not been very difficult—it is balancing the needs of the immigrant community against the collection budget, the buildings in need of renovation and the other audiences that we serve that is always a challenge!"
- "Narrowing down how much can be done realistically; we have become a very popular partner for other departments and organizations."
- "I also do acquisitions, reference, and write and publish—days can be fragmented."
- "Acquiring tenure while working on each of these aspects of the job. Many times these aspects are considered as more service and less scholarly and therefore less valued."

Budget Concerns

The theme of budget concerns related to funding and budgets. At least five librarians commented that there were not enough funds to "hire, expand the collection, or advertise in the appropriate media." The support also was mentioned as missing in the area of funding, unless supplied by grant funds. Eight librarians specifically mentioned that the position needed to have a budget to be able to be more autonomous in the areas of collection development and programming. One librarian indicated that it was important to have "resources to offer and rely on! We have to be ready for specific needs and it's very difficult to have something to offer without a budget."

Contributions of Departments

Many of the individuals in these positions are not associated with any particular department, but rather work individually with connections to other departments. Respondents were asked, "Do you feel that your department contributes positively to your growth?" For this question, many interpreted "department" to mean "administration." Even so, 23.4% of respondents indicated that their department does not contribute to their growth as much as they would like. Hispanic Americans had a higher dissatisfaction percentage at 36.4%. Some of the reasons given for this dissatisfaction included these themes: reluctance to try something new, lack of support, budgetary concerns, and perspectives.

Reluctance to Try Something New

Librarians charged with developing programs and new initiatives need to be innovative, creative, and risk takers. In order to do so, they are investing their time and energies in exploring possibilities. This may contribute to their personal and professional growth, but the goal is that it will also contribute to the growth of other librarians, who may need to reach outside their comfort zone in order to bring in new perspectives and experiences in an attempt to expand their views and competencies. Individuals who challenge the status quo without support may become frustrated and alienated.

Librarians mentioned the struggle they have had in proposing new ideas. Staff reluctance to try something new was one of the main frustrations. Senior staff especially become accustomed to certain patterns or approaches. One librarian shared her aggravation toward the inaction of staff when she would suggest something that might take them out of their comfort zone or that might require a little more effort on their part. She not only found it difficult to find assistance, but also experienced some of the bitterness directed toward her. Another librarian even commented, "This place is sort of like high school, with backbiting and gossiping. Argh." For others, even changing day-to-day routines was a struggle so it became even more of a challenge to suggest anything beyond that. One person shared, "The 'diversity' branch library I am in is very behind the times in regards to library technology and student communication and outreach. Trying to get them to change anything is like pulling teeth."

Need for Risk Takers: Finding a Voice

A common frustration noted by the librarians in the study was that it was difficult to get others to work with them. Some of the comments that emerged when the librarians discussed this point were these:

- There is a lack of an administration statement about the importance of learning how to work effectively with other cultures.
- Individuals don't want to change the way they are currently providing services; there is a sentiment that if they treat everyone the same, that should be good enough;
- They don't have time to make adjustments to what they are doing.
- They are unsure of how they should respond, react, or interact with individuals from other cultures. Perhaps they feel uncomfortable and avoid stepping outside their comfort zone by simply continuing to do what they were doing, since their view is that it was working.

The profession is in need of those who will take the risks and speak out to improve situations and to educate others. Some examples of librarians who fit into this role are identified as "Movers & Shakers" annually by *Library Journal*. These individuals are rewarded for going against the status quo. Oftentimes it is the individual who is not of the mainstream, or who works with individuals from other cultures, or those who are underrepresented, who recognizes the inequities or injustices and strives to effect changes. However, depending upon their approach and the support received, their attempts may be seen as out of line or threatening to others. One exceptional Latina librarian, who fit the role of a "mover and shaker," was ostracized because of her recommendations at one library. If she suggested anything beyond ideas for programming, a murmur would begin among certain staff who were concerned she was going to start talking about discrimination again. Although she was originally motivated to take risks and speak out, she eventually learned to not make waves" and to maintain the status quo.

Another librarian, an African American male, decided to stand up for creating a more diverse exhibit, even though he was at first hoping that he wouldn't be the one to have to say something:

> You can be sitting in a meeting and we can be talking about doing like an exhibit. We were talking about putting some photographs up in the room where all the computers are; to put some pictures on the wall and break it up to beautify the wall. So the person who was doing it said "We're going to put pictures up from the 1920s." So when they put pictures up there it was only white people and white men in the pictures and I'm like "Okay, am I the only one that sees this question?" and I'm just going to wait and I won't have to be the one to say anything. And the meeting went on and on and people said things like "These are great pictures." So finally I couldn't stand it anymore and I said, "You know, I understand what you're trying to do but you have to understand I think we need some people with color and we need women in these pictures. If we're going to create a warm and welcoming environment we need pictures that reflect other groups." And they said, "Well there are no women and no people of color from the pictures we want to pick from this era." And then I said, "We are picking the wrong era then. If the 20's weren't warm and welcoming for women then don't put the pictures on the x-x-wall." We had a big ole fight about this.

In this case the librarian decided to speak up and "go against the grain" because he knew it was important that the library work to represent other cultures and people. However, oftentimes it is an exhausting and emotional uphill battle to get others to see why it is important to work towards developing that cultural sensitivity and to think of the needs of groups outside the mainstream population. The ramifications can be negative if there is not buy-in. However, the rewards include the satisfaction of knowing that diversity is better represented in the library and that perhaps some individuals heard the message. For some, just pointing out the lack of representation would be sufficient to bring them on board. Yet, if individuals do not feel confident to even voice that concern, the status quo can easily persist.

Lack of Support

A common thread that ran through responses, both in the survey and in the interviews, was that there needed to be more support, both from the library administration and the staff, especially when new ideas were proposed. For some, the administration was key in whether or not the efforts would go forward. This is captured by the following comment: "The campus wide library administration has little interest in what the front line library staff has to say and makes almost all decisions without any input from staff and only token efforts at gaining staff buy in."

There were also many comments regarding the lack of support for the position and any efforts made. Twelve individuals wrote remarks stating that once they were in the position they were on their own to make things work. They did not receive much guidance or any support as far as helping the others in the library understand the importance of the position or what the goals were. There did not seem to be many librarians who felt that the staff had a common understanding of the position or the goals, approaches, or visions. Eight librarians also felt that they were perceived as "tokens" in the position and that they were still viewed with doubts or seen as less of a scholar. Politics were cited as another reason that there might not have been as much support as was needed. In many libraries, it is just an added-on duty (such as a subject specialist taking on one more area) that does not carry much support (time or money). This lack of support may be one of the reasons that librarians felt there was a "general desire to maintain status quo."

When asked, "What would you like the library administration to know about this type of position or future positions?" one interviewee shared the following: "I think one of the things, and I guess I touched on it earlier, is it needs some kind of power, but there needs to be a budget. It needs to have some kind of administrative mandate behind it. I don't have a budget for example to buy electronics, but nobody does. So I have to go and fight for getting something like the *Chicago Defender*; to get the subscription for *ProQuest*."

Another librarian remarked, "This is a culture that I stepped into and I don't know why they are like this, or have this commitment to diversity, but I'm thankful that they do because I couldn't work in a place that's not."

Work Satisfaction

Job satisfaction is a dynamic, changing idea that reflects an individual's attitudes and expectations toward his or her work and goals in life (Sherrer, 1985). Vaughn and Dunn (1974) described it as the feeling an employee has about his or her pay, work, promotion opportunities, coworkers, and supervisor. It can also refer to the feelings and emotional aspects of people's experiences toward their jobs, as different from intellectual or rational aspects (Nandy, 1985).

In this study not even two thirds (61.7%) of the respondents said they were satisfied with their job and just over one quarter (27.7%) indicated that sometimes they were satisfied. These percentages were for overall work satisfaction related to their environment, training, support, expectations, respect, isolation (see figure 4.2). These results are a bit lower than those of a national study of librarian job satisfaction published in 2008. In that study, Topper (2008) reported that of the 1,209 respondents (not restricted to job class, type, age, or ethnicity), about 70% reported being either "very satisfied" (32.1%) or "satisfied" (37.9%) with their jobs. Just under a quarter reported they were "some-

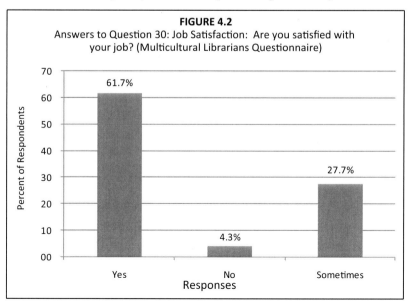

FIGURE 4.2
Answers to Question 30: Job Satisfaction: Are you satisfied with your job? (Multicultural Librarians Questionnaire)

what satisfied" (23.4%). Only 6.7% admitted they were dissatisfied with their career choice.

There are many variables and circumstances that contribute to job satisfaction. In this study the focus was on aspects that might be specific to working with diverse populations. Because these librarians are working with ethnic groups and many have positions that put them outside of the norm, it seems appropriate to compare the experiences here to those of other librarians who are either of ethnic descent or working with ethnic populations.

In a study done in 2000, Thornton found that more than 70% of the librarians of African American descent who responded to a survey were satisfied with the range of their occupational tasks, autonomy, variety of challenges, professional development, working conditions, and their position as role models (pp. 226–227). Reasons for dissatisfaction included: "(1) threatening, oppressive environment, (2) lack of respect and acceptance by colleagues and library administration for contribution to the organization, (3) few African American librarians, (4) isolation, (5) racism..." (pp. 229–230). This study also found that that these same conditions were causes for some dissatisfaction, especially the lack of respect and acceptance and the sense of isolation. In a study done by Dilevko (2004), tribal college workers were interviewed, and they also felt that it was important to have a sense of autonomy and to serve as role models (and to be respected). Several authors have written about the concerns for job satisfaction of librarians of non-Anglo ethnic descent, especially related to isolation, lack of respect and a feeling that they are token hires (Ruan & Xiong, 2008; Dilevko & Gottlieb, 2004; Thornton, 2000; Squire, 1991).

This survey asked several similar questions related to job satisfaction, including autonomy on the job, workload, interaction with peers, opportunities for professional development, proportion of faculty of non-Anglo ethnic descent, respect for knowledge, isolation on the job, trying to fit into the work environment, unsupported at work, experience of racial discrimination, that the administration has a commitment to diversity. These will be discussed below with comparisons made to Thornton's study for various categories.

Autonomy

For the most part, the librarians surveyed were either very satisfied or satisfied with the autonomy on the job (see figure 4.3). The other responses did not include such high ratings so they will be presented separately.

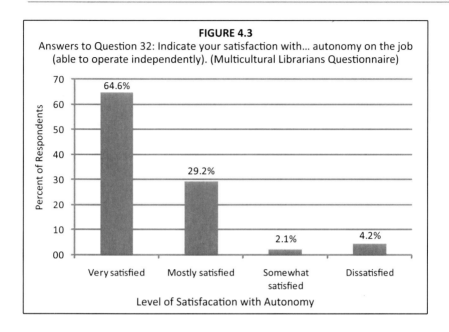

FIGURE 4.3
Answers to Question 32: Indicate your satisfaction with... autonomy on the job (able to operate independently). (Multicultural Librarians Questionnaire)

Although most librarians surveyed felt satisfied with their autonomy on the job, some felt a sense that they had to prove what they could do without the support they felt was needed. Following is an example of some of the negative consequences of having too much autonomy:

> My orientation was very general in terms of the library. I really believe I was left to my own devices to the multicultural part with the understanding to do whatever I wanted to do and what ever avenues [and that I] would be supported by the library. Now, a couple of years ago to three years ago, the library formed the diversity committee specifically made up of librarians and staff to find ways that we can better serve first populations on this campus. So I'm just learning what's going on and it's taking a little while to get off the ground.

Another librarian felt that he didn't have enough autonomy and remarked, "My position should have the autonomy necessary to have an impact with hiring, collection development, technology acquisition, and a separate budget."

Workload

When asked about satisfaction with workload, only 17% said they were very satisfied (see figure 4.4). It would be good to get a pulse on the general field of librarianship and how that question would be ranked. Are librarians in these positions generally less satisfied than the norm?

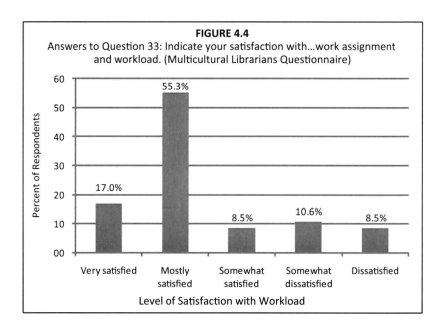

FIGURE 4.4

Answers to Question 33: Indicate your satisfaction with...work assignment and workload. (Multicultural Librarians Questionnaire)

From the present survey one respondent remarked, "It's been interesting to fill this survey, as I am contemplating changing careers after over 13 years of service simply because the workload is impacting my family and children. I do love this job and will look to serve still the same population, although at a different level."

Interaction with Peers

When considering satisfaction with interaction with peers, over three quarters of the respondents indicated that they were either mostly or very satisfied (see figure 4.5).

Although a high percentage of librarians surveyed were satisfied with the collegiality and working relationships they had with their peers, there was some dissatisfaction. Some of this resulted from the negative atmosphere caused due to the backbiting, the gossiping, and the ever-present shadow of library politics. Others remarked that certain subject specialists

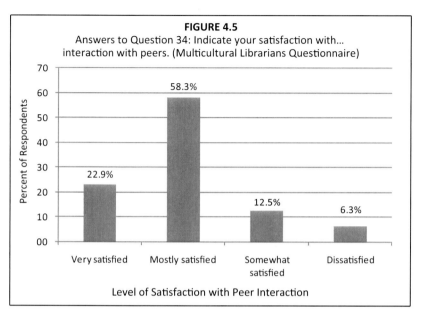

FIGURE 4.5
Answers to Question 34: Indicate your satisfaction with...
interaction with peers. (Multicultural Librarians Questionnaire)

were territorial and did not feel that students or faculty in areas covered by their subject collections should be going to the multicultural librarian for help. One Latina librarian who was the outreach librarian was approached frequently by the Latino students and faculty on campus because she was warm, open, caring, and very service oriented. But the Latin American bibliographer was very territorial because he felt the students who went to her should instead come to him for reference assistance because he was a subject specialist. Rather than both working together to serve this constituency, it became a contentious situation.

This type of territorial struggle was echoed by another librarian, an African American male:

> Folks in academia are very territorial. As soon as they think you're infringing on their territory, like I go over to the medical library to start to talk about stuff on minority health issues, they get really oversensitive. It's more of a kind of collegial kind of thing that you need to be able to initiate with the medical Library and I think people in public libraries are used to that kind of negotiation and outreach with, I don't want to say hostile people, but they deal with that kind of stuff every day. I think a lot of library administrators and HR people are saying they

don't have that experience in academic libraries. Yet when
I suggested ways to be more inclusive in the collections
or in their publicity they got defensive.

Someone needs to look at collections, displays, print, and online information from the perspectives of students of color to determine if these resources are meeting their needs and are representative of those being served, regardless of color, culture, disability, or ability. Collection development and liaison duties are huge responsibilities, and working collaboratively toward a common goal is the desirable outcome.

Another librarian had positive interactions with subject librarians and remarked:

If students have a specific research question or need related to Native American studies I have made sure they know that they don't have to talk to me. And I think that helps that we are a small library and we're warm and approachable. It hasn't been any of that territorial aspect and I'm really glad because I think when you're working with multicultural groups you can't have that. The point is to help these people to use a library, and you can't be defensive of your turf. A larger picture is that we're all here for the same purpose and I think that's how we have to approach any kind of multicultural service.

Professional Opportunities

In fact, having multiple librarians to help serve various populations has the advantage of reducing the feeling of isolation, as well as creating a team effort in terms of collaborating with other librarians about approaches and collections and services. Many of the librarians surveyed also relied heavily on networks they used throughout the country to help them professionally. Over three quarters of the respondents indicated that they were either very or mostly satisfied with their opportunities for professional development (see figure 4.6).

Although the librarians had opportunities to attend conferences and workshops, they still mentioned the need to have more professional

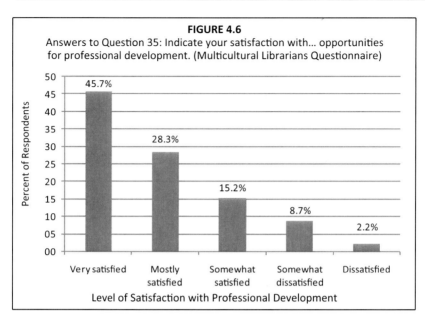

FIGURE 4.6
Answers to Question 35: Indicate your satisfaction with... opportunities for professional development. (Multicultural Librarians Questionnaire)

engagement with other librarians working in similar roles. Two specific comments related to this issue were these:

- "It definitely would help to have an active network of librarians that work with multicultural services."
- "I would love to build a stronger network of colleagues working in Academic Libraries. Sometimes I think we are all over worked and thus have no time to build those relationships."

Faculty of Color

Recruitment and retention are areas of great effort on campuses and within libraries, yet the percentage of library faculty of color is still extremely small. For this study, faculty of color includes faculty of non-Anglo ethnic descent, especially including faculty of Hispanic, African American, Native American and Asian descent. This small representation may lead to isolation and feelings of being targeted. It should be no surprise that most were not satisfied with the ethnic representation (see figure 4.7).

Thornton's study (2000) indicated that respondents were dissatisfied to very dissatisfied with the proportion of faculty of African descent in the library (79.4%) and at the institution (75.7%). The present study did not specify any particular ethnic group or whether at the library or the institution. Even so, 60.4% in this study also indicated that they were somewhat dissatisfied to dissatisfied with the proportion of faculty of color (figure 4.7).

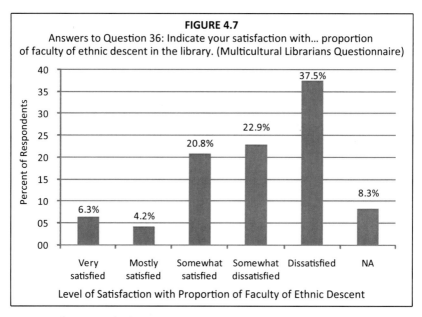

FIGURE 4.7

Answers to Question 36: Indicate your satisfaction with… proportion of faculty of ethnic descent in the library. (Multicultural Librarians Questionnaire)

Respect for Knowledge

Another question related to work environment satisfaction was whether these librarians felt there was respect for their knowledge. In Thornton's study (2000), 82% of the respondents felt moderately or to a high degree that their knowledge was respected, which is almost identical to this study (82.6% in the same categories; see figure 4.8).

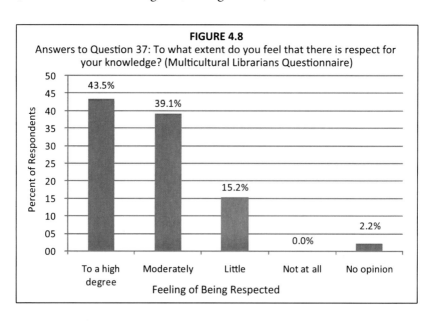

FIGURE 4.8

Answers to Question 37: To what extent do you feel that there is respect for your knowledge? (Multicultural Librarians Questionnaire)

However, if we combine the statistics a different way we see that 54.30% (over half) of the respondents to the present survey indicated that they felt there was little or only moderate respect for their knowledge. When this question is compared with ethnicity, 83% of the white Anglo Americans indicated they felt respected to a high degree or moderately. In contrast, only 50% of the Hispanic Americans indicated they felt respected to a high degree or moderately.

Many of the comments related to this question were that there did not seem to be much acknowledgement of the value of the position or of the person's duties. One respondent, who had been in the position for 13 years, said, "Even after reaching this position, I'm simply seen as an implementer and not as someone with a larger scope of understanding."

Another librarian felt that what she did was not valued because people did not understand what her role was. She felt that many thought that all she did was "socialize." Because many of these positions are newly created, they do not have the history of people being able to point to something concrete that has been done. She felt that it was hard to document and explain to others the value of the work she was doing in her outreach capacity. Her suggestion was to provide reports to the library staff, perhaps a newsletter of accomplishments, so the staff could begin to see the type of work being done and perhaps the impact.

Tokenism

If librarians feel that they are perceived as having gotten a position solely based on their ethnic background, they no doubt will face added tensions in a job. In this study, some librarians did report that they felt that they were not respected for their knowledge or abilities. One librarian did not feel as though she was afforded the opportunity to reach her full potential and was selected only because of her ability to speak Spanish. She remarked, "I feel the system uses me to provide services to the Spanish speaking. I feel that I am a 'TOKEN.'" Another librarian, who had developed extraordinary cultural programs at a research library, eventually transitioned away from her outreach position because she felt she was being ridiculed for her efforts. She did not feel that others appreciated her efforts and that some of her colleagues only tolerated her efforts or else dismissed her, saying that she was hired only because she was a minority. These were her perceptions, but they were so strong that it was clear in the telling that after a number of years in that environment she learned to keep her distance. Although she was highly qualified and is nationally respected for her efforts, initiative, and voice, many individuals at her own institution were unable to get past the feeling that she was hired as a "target of opportunity." Her self-esteem and drive were damaged in the process.

Isolation

Thornton's (2000) study of African American librarians revealed that 34.5% perceived a moderate to high degree of isolation in the workplace. This study indicated that 37.8% of the African Americans perceived a moderate to high degree of isolation, with 42.6% of all respondents in this study indicating a feeling of isolation (see figure 4.9).

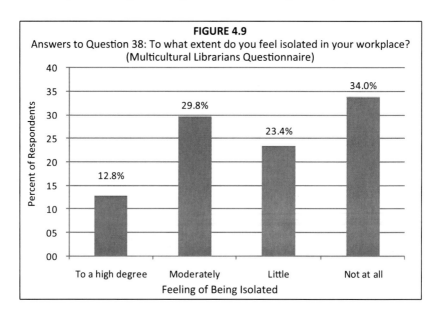

FIGURE 4.9
Answers to Question 38: To what extent do you feel isolated in your workplace? (Multicultural Librarians Questionnaire)

Interestingly, the white Anglo Americans and the Hispanic Americans felt the greatest isolation. It would be good to delve into this question more to determine how these groups differed in their views of isolation and how it was manifested.

Fitting In

If a librarian is from a culture outside the mainstream culture, it may be difficult to get connected and to gain admittance into an environment, even a work environment with established cultures, norms, and expectations. More than a third of the respondents (39.1%) felt either to a high degree or moderately that they needed to try to fit into their work environment (see figure 4.10).

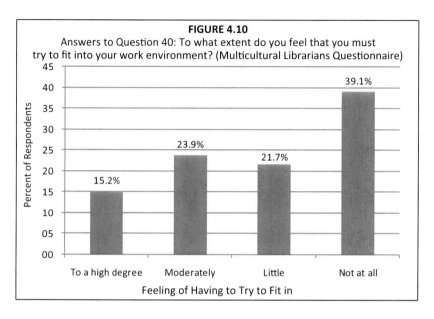

FIGURE 4.10

Answers to Question 40: To what extent do you feel that you must try to fit into your work environment? (Multicultural Librarians Questionnaire)

However, when this question was compared with ethnicity, the results showed that none of the white Anglo American librarians selected "To a high degree," whereas 50% of the Hispanic Americans and 33.3% of the African Americans did. On the flip side, the white Anglo American librarians experienced that difficulty of fitting into the environment outside of the library when they tried to gain an entrée into the various cultural groups. In those instances, the white librarians were then not of the mainstream population. They experienced in reverse what people of color may experience in a white-dominated library environment.

Power Struggles

Oftentimes librarians from cultures outside of the mainstream, or those who work with different cultures, have different approaches and perspectives than mainstream librarians. Howland (2001) points out that working in a multicultural environment is invariably complex and challenging because of "fluctuating power dynamics" and the need for staff members to merge "a diversity of opinions and approaches" (p. 105). They come with varied background experiences, expectations, attitudes, perspectives, and styles, which may threaten established staff who may want to maintain the status quo. Howland also notes that they may "fear an erosion of their personal institutional power and/or to fear power shifts throughout the organization that may have a negative impact upon them" (p.105). These non-mainstream librarians may also have taken courses or training in social justice or multicultural education and understand the importance of challenging the norm or suggesting ways to improve the cultural awareness of others. Finding a voice is one of the important ways that an individual can help to make change, yet knowing how and when to express different views is a skill.

Conversations with a Latina librarian concerning her power struggles as outreach librarian at her academic research library painted a grim picture. It seemed that at every turn her efforts were being halted by individuals on the senior management group who felt that she was trying to use discrimination as a tool for forcing the administration to try different approaches. The library advocates who had originally recommended the creation of the position and who recruited her had since left the library. The power had shifted to others who did not have the same understanding of the importance of what she had already accomplished and what she was striving to promote.

Lack of Support

The above examples provide some insight of how some librarians feel isolated and unsupported in their work environment. Figure 4.11 provides a

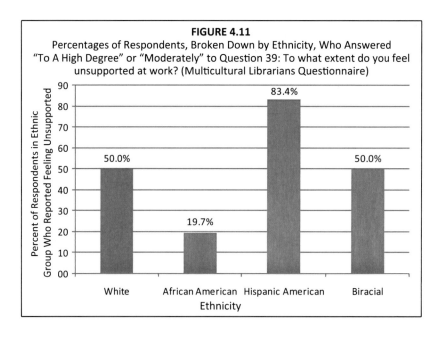

FIGURE 4.11
Percentages of Respondents, Broken Down by Ethnicity, Who Answered "To A High Degree" or "Moderately" to Question 39: To what extent do you feel unsupported at work? (Multicultural Librarians Questionnaire)

breakdown by ethnicity of percentages of individuals who felt unsupported either to a high degree or moderately. Hispanic Americans indicated the highest degree of feeling unsupported (83.4%)

Thornton's study (2000), however, summarized that the overall response was that all librarians felt supported at work. In this study, however, various ethnic groups indicated they felt little support. It is important to recognize, though, that this study was surveying librarians in roles as multicultural services librarians, so the concept of support may have different interpretations here. It may be that the individuals themselves felt supported, but they felt little support for carrying out the work related to this position. Over three quarters of the respondents felt they were not being supported either to a high or moderate degree. This frustration may be one reason individuals in these positions leave. It would be valuable to locate more librarians who left these positions to determine if this was one reason for leaving. Conversations with several librarians at conferences who had either worked in this capacity and had left or who knew others who did revealed that some reasons for leaving were lack of support, work overload, not feeling a part of the community, and not feeling that their work was appreciated.

In the example of the Latina librarian who was unable to find a workable method to communicate ideas and perspectives, according to her observations, there was no merging of opinions and approaches. Instead, she indicated that each party held firmly to their original viewpoint. Because of different communication styles, the Latina librarian was seen as being pushy and demanding. However, she felt that the involved parties were being unresponsive and not open to even listening to new ideas. Had there been someone to look at the interaction in an objective way, to extract the ideas and restate them in a way that was not threatening to either party, some headway might have been made. However, expecting a "translator" is not realistic. Instead, all parties would be better served to have a better understanding of different communication styles so that they don't feel attacked or threatened. In this case, the librarian felt that she was unsupported and that here efforts were made in vain.

Experiences with Racial Discrimination

The preceding example is one instance of how librarians may feel discrimination. A question in the survey asked about experiences with discrimination. This topic was not intentionally discussed in interviews, and few comments in the survey related to this problem. Discrimination was not defined, nor were there examples given of what discrimination might look like on the job. Figure 4.12 provides a breakdown of the extent that these librarians experienced incidences of racial discrimination. Over 38% said they had not experienced it at all. In past workshops conducted, the author experienced similar results of many initially indicating they had not experienced discrimination (either personally or witnessed) or didn't know if they had. Once individuals began sharing subtle ways people witness discrimination (even as subtle as ethnic jokes or exclusion or avoidance), virtually everyone could recall ways they had experienced discrimination.

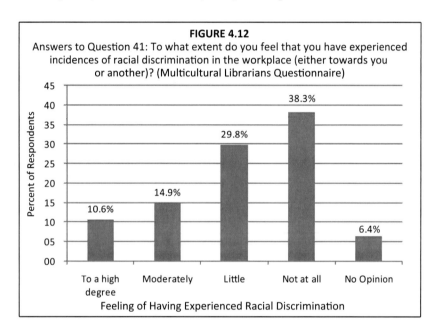

FIGURE 4.12

Answers to Question 41: To what extent do you feel that you have experienced incidences of racial discrimination in the workplace (either towards you or another)? (Multicultural Librarians Questionnaire)

Thornton's study (2000) revealed that 26% of the respondents had experienced incidences of racial discrimination in the workplace. This study was similar in reporting 25.5% across all groups (in the moderately to a high degree category). When compared with ethnicity a different picture emerges (see figure 4.13).

In this figure, the percentages shift considerably to indicate that more than half of the African and Hispanic Americans had experienced discrimination to a high or moderate degree. One comment from the present study related to possible discrimination was, "It is a difficult job! There are no chances of promotion. Despite 15 years of working for the

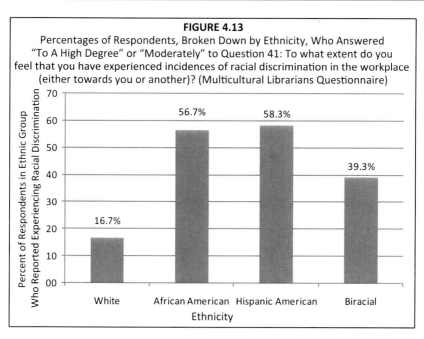

FIGURE 4.13
Percentages of Respondents, Broken Down by Ethnicity, Who Answered
"To A High Degree" or "Moderately" to Question 41: To what extent do you
feel that you have experienced incidences of racial discrimination in the workplace
(either towards you or another)? (Multicultural Librarians Questionnaire)

system, when management jobs become available administration seeks 'white' employees from outside the system and the excuse is that they need to bring 'new blood.'"

Library Commitment to Diversity

Many of these librarians experienced isolation, power struggles, difficulty fitting into the environment, and overt discrimination. One of their tasks is to work with the library administration and staff to eliminate these negative work conditions, as well as to create an environment that is more inclusive and welcoming. In order to accomplish this task, they need support from the administration and a strong institutional commitment to diversity. Almost three quarters of the respondents felt their libraries had either a high or moderate commitment to diversity, as represented in figure 4.14.

In this study, a combined total of 72.4% of the respondents felt that the administration is committed to diversity either moderately or to a high degree. Going again to Thornton's study (2000), 52% of those respondents indicated that the administration was committed somewhat or a high degree to diversity. Given that these studies were done seven years apart, this is a positive trend: there appears to be the perception that the administration is more committed now to diversity. Granted, there is no

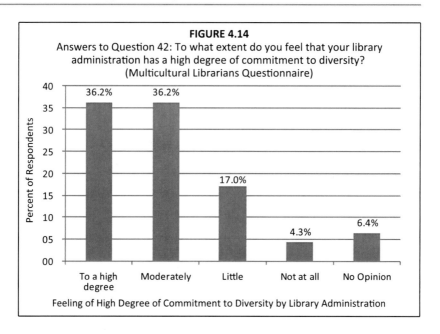

FIGURE 4.14
Answers to Question 42: To what extent do you feel that your library administration has a high degree of commitment to diversity? (Multicultural Librarians Questionnaire)

Feeling of High Degree of Commitment to Diversity by Library Administration

way to know if the librarians surveyed were from similar institutions, yet both studies were done with librarians from a wide geographic area. Yet if responses are separated out by ethnicity, the results are not as high, with white Anglo Americans providing much higher scoring than any of the other ethnic groups. Because Thornton's study did not break out responses by ethnicity, it is difficult to examine this trend as a function of ethnicity.

Overall, in Thornton's study respondents were most satisfied with job duties, variety of occupational tasks, interaction with patrons, autonomy, challenges of the job, working conditions, professional development, and job security. Those findings are very similar to findings from this current study. Even though this study was smaller in scope, the issues seem to be pretty consistent even several years after Thornton's study.

Additional Comments

In the present study many librarians offered additional comments related to the question of job satisfaction. Combinations such as "rewarding and frustrating" or "satisfying and overworked" were common. One librarian remarked, "One difficulty is once you have been a multicultural librarian and find that you like the work, but not the job you have, it is hard to find a new job. There really aren't many (at least in academic libraries) so you are stuck waiting for one to pop up in a place you could stand to live and at an acceptable salary." Another said, "It helps to remember that life itself is a 'process of becoming' and this field of librarianship is one of constant change, challenge and opportunity. In this position, you need to have a highly developed sense of diplomacy, political savvy and persistence."

Suggestions

Librarians who were interviewed provided some suggestions that might help librarians during the hiring process and in the initial phases of the job:

- Negotiate which aspects of the job description you feel are realistic and possibly rework the job description indicating primary duties and additional duties as time permits. It may be helpful to have some understanding of who else will be working on these initiatives at the library so that a team is present at the beginning.
- Negotiate during the hiring process to get a budget for programming and collection development for ethnic studies areas that may not be part of the regular subject specialist's workflow. Explain the importance of having a budget line for a student to help with programming, publicity, documentation efforts for training, and outreach endeavors.
- Negotiate some funding to be able to attend a couple of diversity conferences each year, indicating the difficulty in networking with other librarians in similar positions, as well as to receive concentrated training and examples.
- Get a commitment by the library administration to have an open meeting where you will be introduced with the administration providing an introduction or orientation to the importance of the work that you will be conducting and the need for library participation.
- Find other librarians in the library who are also interested in the populations you will serve and work together to develop strategies for how you can create a team approach for reference, consultations, referrals, outreach, and collection building.

Summary

Some of the best work occurs when there are differing viewpoints and approaches at the table. Yet, this can be threatening to some individuals. Librarians in positions that serve diverse populations need to have the flexibility of working with multiple constituencies and feeling as though they are supported in their efforts. It can be unsettling if these librarians approach colleagues to work collaboratively and instead of cooperation meet resistance. Because change is not always appreciated, librarians serving diverse populations may find it difficult to fit into their environment if they are proposing a different way to look at how people interact or provide services. Librarians in this study offered their insights of the need for a supportive administration, as well as suggestions for creating a more realistic job description and approach to the position.

CHAPTER FIVE

Getting Started

Getting started in a job that might be newly created or that has a vague or overambitious job description was a major concern of many of the librarians who participated in this study. This concern was also voiced by librarians during informal conversations at conferences. These librarians also felt that it is important for librarians with little prior knowledge or experience to have some guidance in how to become culturally competent. Some of the questions they had when first starting out were these.

How do librarians learn to

- work with diverse cultures?
- initiate, coordinate, and expand diversity-related programs at their libraries and institutions?
- gain an entrée as liaisons to their various diverse populations?
- better prepare all librarians to be culturally competent?

This chapter will provide suggestions for getting started in a position, including creating a plan of action (which differs from an action plan), gaining an entrée into various communities, and developing campus support.

There are many challenges in working in a multicultural environment. The previous chapter described some of the challenges related to balancing responsibilities, budget concerns, job satisfaction, and support issues. Howland (2001) provided an excellent overview of some of the challenges that libraries face with regard to creating a multicultural environment, including fluctuating power dynamics, managing a diversity of opinions and approaches, overcoming a perceived lack of empathy, tokenism (real or perceived), holding everyone throughout the organization accountable for achieving a positive multicultural environment, and turning challenges into opportunities. Although Howland may have directed the article more at administrators, all of these challenges were experienced by the librarians in this study, some to higher degrees than others. Some of the librarians found ways to overcome the challenges. Because so few librarians are in these roles to begin with, library administrators need to be cognizant of ways to create a more inclusive environment. Some of this means becoming educated about and aware of the issues and challenges. It also means being flexible in allowing for different methods and approaches. Administrators also need to set the tone from the beginning and throughout that these positions are valued, integral parts of the library.

This chapter presents some of the suggestions for moving past barriers. It will first provide survey results for how respondents approached various aspects of their job and will then provide some guidelines for getting started in a position and establishing relationships.

Working to Achieve a Multicultural Environment
Setting Priorities

In chapter 4, librarians surveyed indicated that their job description included so much that it was difficult for them to do justice to all the tasks. Setting priorities was difficult for many because they felt everything needed to be done immediately. After discussing with various librarians what they believed were the critical components of their job, four areas rose to the top: establishing relationships, becoming a presence in the library or community, developing a plan of action, and developing an

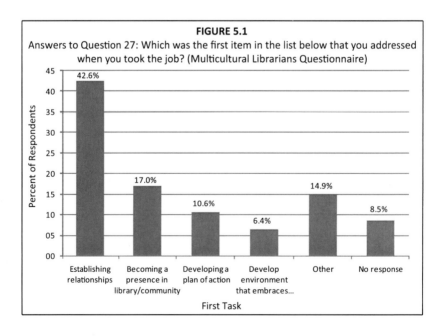

FIGURE 5.1

Answers to Question 27: Which was the first item in the list below that you addressed when you took the job? (Multicultural Librarians Questionnaire)

environment that embraces diversity. Although there are additional important components, these four areas were presented as goals that most librarians in these positions felt they needed to accomplish. Of these four areas, librarians surveyed indicated which one they first addressed (see figure 5.1).

Establishing relationships was indicated by almost 43% of the librarians (for all groups averaged together) as the first task they addressed. Table 5.1 shows the first tasks by ethnicity.

Table 5.1
Answers Most Often Chosen to Question 27, Broken Down by Ethnicity: Which was the first item in the list below that you addressed when you took the job? (Multicultural Librarians Questionnaire)

Ethnicity	First Task
White Anglo Americans	Develop a plan of action
African Americans	Becoming a presence in the library/ community
Asian Americans	Establishing relationships
Native Americans	Becoming a presence in the community
Hispanic Americans	Other
Other (biracial)	Develop an environment that embraces diversity

Other Comments
Six librarians commented that they really couldn't focus on just one issue, but felt they needed to address all areas simultaneously, especially because the issues were all interconnected. Two librarians shared the need to learn first about the library culture and "being patient with negative perceptions from my own bosses." Another librarian remarked that her first priority was "figuring out what the mountain of stuff on my desk was all about." In her case, a person in the position had left "stuff" but without any clear explanation of what it was, what needed to be done, or what had been done before. Knowing where to begin was one of the major challenges for most of the librarians in these positions.

Working with Other Cultures
The next question on the survey asked about challenges of working with diverse cultures (see figure 5.2).

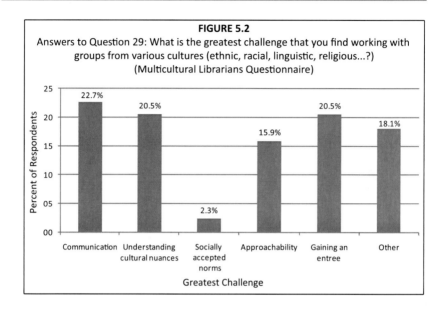

FIGURE 5.2

Answers to Question 29: What is the greatest challenge that you find working with groups from various cultures (ethnic, racial, linguistic, religious...?) (Multicultural Librarians Questionnaire)

Here again, the average for all groups presents a different picture than answers broken out by ethnicity. Three of the groups, the white Anglo Americans, the African Americans, and the other (biracial) respondents had clusters of responses that indicated a spread in the greatest challenge, similar to what is presented in figure 5.2. The Asian American, however, clearly marked socially accepted norms as the greatest challenge (100%), and the Hispanic Americans' first choice was other (50%).

Specific Comments

There were many added comments to the above question. One challenge that librarians felt made the job difficult was the constant shifting of the student population and of staff in departments on campus. Because enrollment and positions change year to year, they have to figure out the level of research sophistication and level of need on a regular basis, not only means for the students, but also for the contacts (staff and faculty liaisons) throughout the campus. A librarian mentioned that "the amount of turnover on the other ends" made it "difficult to keep the relationship going."

Another element noted as impacting the job was not having enough time. The ability to effectively connect with others was hindered due to time constraints as well. Because of all of the other duties assigned, librarians felt they did not have the time to connect with everyone. They also felt that because they had to prioritize their work, oftentimes the time needed to learn more about other cultures or to go out to the departments and other areas to connect with students and faculty was used for other in-house duties, like reference, instruction, collection development, and meetings. Yet one of the main challenges mentioned by one librarian was "getting the groups to be interested in the library." If one of the goals of this position is to increase that connection and to help the students who are typically underserved know about the library, then it seems that connecting should be placed much higher on the priority list. Connecting especially to the "at-risk" populations and assisting them with library research can help efforts to retain these students.

One librarian said that she did not have any challenges because "I am sensitive to everyone's needs." Unless this person has been raised in hundreds of cultures, religions, disabilities, languages, and ethnicities, it seems very unlikely that this person could be sensitive to everyone's needs. Because a person has received some sensitivity training or has been raised in a culture or language from an underrepresented group does not make that individual equally able to understand all cultures, languages, norms, or modes of communication preferences. Hopefully this individual doesn't also make comments such as "I treat everyone the same" or "I'm color blind to differences in skin color." Each culture is distinct. What is acceptable with one may not work for another. In fact, even within cultures there are so many variables. If the librarian meant that she respects each individual, that is wonderful. Each of us, however, must have various challenges when working with any other individual, and part of becoming culturally competent is to recognize our strengths, weaknesses, biases, and areas in need of improvement.

Guidelines for Getting Started

The remainder of this chapter will provide some suggestions for how to approach the various components of a job that serves diverse populations. It takes into account some of the major areas of concern by the librarians in this study: establishing relationships, becoming a presence in the community, and developing a plan of action.

Start by Determining What Has Already Been Done

As previously indicated, most librarians entered this position without a lot of training or personal knowledge of how to approach the work, unless they had been residents or interns in a similar position. Many librarians felt that it was important to get their house in order before they could even begin to think of tackling anything else. Once this task was done, they could then take a look at what else had been done through library committees and departments related to diversity. Although this first step can be quite time-consuming, it sets up many of the elements that would be covered next in the job, including creating contacts and a plan of action. Following are some suggestions for determining what has already been done.

Organize Files

Make an account of computer and paper files that exist from any previous person in this position and organize by subjects that make sense to you. Make files for these categories:

- Contacts on campus and in the community. Transfer any notes previously made related to those contacts.
- Events done in the past and notes about improvements for the future. Are any handouts or promotional materials available, or the distribution list for the promotional materials? Are there notes about the planning process, timeline, presenters, and cost? Was any feedback gathered?
- Exhibits (by date). Look for past exhibits related to diversity issues, including who was responsible, partners and resources used, and feedback.
- Partners on campus. Who are the key partners for each program and how do they want information communicated to them?
- Partners from the community. Who are the resources for the various populations? Include contact information, plans for programs, and outreach.
- Grants. What grants have been applied for, are being considered, or iare n process? Are there already lists of sources for grants (online or in print) and typical deadlines each year?
- Committees related to diversity. Consult minutes of committee meetings to see what has previously been discussed related to diversity issues. It may be obvious to look at the diversity, outreach, exhibit, and programming committees. However, look also at executive or library departmental or advisory committee minutes.

- Diversity, outreach, and public engagement committees. Read these minutes and plans carefully, looking for accomplishments as well as partners, action plans, and goals.
- Exhibit committee. Track exhibits from past years to see how diversity has been represented. Is there a plan for including diversity elements in each exhibit, or is it only the heroes and holidays approach? Has there been an attempt to work with student groups and organizations across campus to infuse their perspective and work in the exhibits?
- Programming committee. If there is no such committee, see if some group tracks programs. Various departments or libraries on campus may have done programming that has not been recorded librarywide. Tag those items related to diversity, as well as partners.
- Publicity. Is there a list (possibly from public relations) of contacts for local media, such as newspapers, newsletters, flyers, radio, magazines. and TV? Are there also media produced for the non-English-speaking communities? This list can be invaluable when promoting activities, exhibits, and programming.
- Library minutes: Consult library, departmental, and division minutes to see if there have been discussions about training, service, or barriers that need to be addressed. Also see if there are annual reports or library director "state of the library" talks where diversity has been discussed with highlights of ways the library has worked towards achieving an inclusive environment.

Assess Collections

To determine priorities and needs for collection development, try to find answer to the following questions: Have there been conversations about addressing the needs of diverse populations through collections? Who covers the small presses that aren't usually picked up through approval plans? These can be rich sources for literature specific to multicultural populations. Have there been conversations related to obtaining databases or online sources geared to diverse cultures? Who is looking at collecting materials related to student recruitment and retention? Has there been an assessment done of the areas of the collection related to your area?

Identify Possibilities for Reference and Instruction Services

Connecting with individuals and groups to help them learn to use the library's resources can be a major aspect of this job. There may be the obvious groups from the cultural houses or support groups to put on a list, but also consider working with subject librarians or the instruction coordinator to determine if you might be able to assist in any of the following areas: classes or topics related to ethnicities, disabilities, diversity, or social justice. Also consider the research areas of faculty within these areas or classes listed related to these topics. These would be potential contacts for providing specific reference or instructional guides, classes, or consultations.

Gather Available Assessment Reports

Chances are that there has been some data gathering and assessment done that will help you determine areas that you would like to target. Try to locate suggestions made to the library by patrons, either in print or online, of improvements they would like to see. Look for surveys, interviews, polls, or focus groups conducted related to library climate or service. See if the responses that touch upon diversity, communication, or interaction suggestions have been pulled into a single file. If not, that process could be suggested. The results could be used to see if there are common needs that are not being addressed

Look at Past Training Efforts

Compiling past training efforts will assist in knowing areas that can be enhanced or strengthened without duplicating programs. Document if the training was done in house, through campus, or external groups. Find out if there is a chronology available of the training, as well as each topic, presenters, cost, handouts, and number of attendees. If not, one can be started. Look at any feedback that was provided from the training sessions. Create computer folders for handouts, presentation slides, and promotional materials.

Review Relevant Campus Groups and Committee Minutes

Look at minutes from campus groups and committees to see how the library has been or could be involved in helping to promote diversity or inclusiveness. Are librarians on these committees? Are there designated library liaisons for each student organization, support group, and cultural house?

Create a Plan of Action

After assessing their situation, many librarians (42.6%) developed plans of action for what they would focus on in the short and long term. This plan of action is a guide for priorities for the position. Some respondent's initial priorities were made easier if a librarian had previously held the position. However, 36% of these positions were newly created, and others entered a position where the person who had left didn't leave a lot of material or hadn't provided information about contacts on campus. A librarian who entered her position after the previous person left said:

> I had very little information in what was there or even from a supervisor about what my predecessor did. But there are a lot of people here on campus who are working on diversity and multicultural issues. For some reason they were all very isolated. So part of what I did was spend time going through the university website trying to track down all of the offices and programs that could work with diversity. That was fairly easy because the departments that liaison with ethnic studies and cultural studies in some way also listed their student group and faculties. That was easy. But I haven't been here a full academic semester so in the fall what I'm hoping to do is really track down some of the groups on campus, and make connections with them face-to-face. I've had very good luck with a few offices on campus. Generally that spirals into something else. The networking is a huge part of it. So often someone in a different office is doing the same thing. I've been able to connect that way and found that they have been helpful, but there weren't a lot of entities that my predecessor worked with.

For many, getting started meant identifying their constituencies and gaining an entrée. The next section will provide some suggestions for areas to consider in a plan of action, such as establishing relationships (library, campus, and community); learning about students' cultures; gaining an entrée; and assessing and developing appropriate collections.

Establish Relationships

After establishing a list of potential committees, departments, groups, organizations, and contacts, the next step would be to make introductions.

Library Relationships

Library staff. Common remarks by librarians in positions that coordinate diversity efforts are that they do not feel staff members understand what they do. It is important to provide information not only about the goals of the position, but also about how you hope to involve others. One African American librarian shared how she introduced herself: "I guess my advice would be, especially as a new person, let people know who you are. Have an open forum and let people hear your story. I shared with them basically my heart and I think it would be helpful for someone who was not from the cultural ethnic group to do that so that people knew who this person was and what their goals were, what they really feel."

Committees. Oftentimes the librarian for multicultural services is placed on the diversity or outreach committee, if one exists, or is asked to create one. Assuming there is a diversity committee (and it was possible to find only 35 ARL libraries with diversity committees), it is important to create rapport with the existing members. The fact that they are on the committee suggests that they are allies and understand the importance of building an inclusive environment. They may have been instrumental in much that has already developed. To gain their support, it might be prudent to acknowledge the work they have done and let them know you are seeking their guidance. It is important to take in the wisdom of what they have learned, not only about the library culture, but also about the work they have done, contacts made, and administrative support. If possible, find someone on the committee who might act as a mentor, someone whom you can consult for advice when you run into a snag or a roadblock and take a coffee break from time to time to discuss matters.

Campus Relationships

Developing campus connections is a major component of networking that is needed for this job. It may be that there are lists available for the stakeholders in the various areas of interest to your efforts. Advice from a female African American librarian regarding this process was to take time to listen to their stories:

Definitely get to people on the campus who are decision makers. Find out who the key people dealing
with diversity on the main campus are, be it African-
American or Hispanic American and let them know
what you are doing, and find out how they feel things
are working in a library or not working; what they
expect. Initially I listen to a lot of people's stories and
for people who weren't sure where they stood with
diversity. I listen to them. Just to hear their concerns,
especially the people who might be on the other side of
the fence or not in support of diversity. I talked with
them and heard their stories and comments. I think
it's really good to do.

A Latina librarian had another strategy that she used to get to know
her faculty:

I've even made a spreadsheet of all my faculty and they
have little bios with pictures so I can recognize them.
My office is by the E area in the reference section. That is
so perfect because that's the section many of my faculty
gravitate to. So when they walk by I say, "Hey are you
so and so?" and they say, "Yes," and then I invite them
in and we chat. They were very flattered that I recognized them. After that connection they talk with their
colleagues and say, "Hey she recognized me." Maybe
that won't work for everyone, but I'm very much, "Hey,
Hey..." that personal interaction. That might be my
personality and the fact that I'm very chatty and social.
That might be helpful for someone. You have to kind of
throw yourself out there.

Another interviewee mentioned, "This position goes beyond reference and programming activities. The person in this position needs to
constantly search for strategic partnerships within the local community,
identify local resources outside of the beaten path and be highly visible—in a way that does not include newspaper articles or TV interviews
on English media."

In addition to establishing contacts with faculty in subject disciplines, other, perhaps obvious networks would be with departments, administrative offices, program houses, and other administrators who work closely with students; including the African American studies department, Latino/Hispanic American department, Native American department, Asian American department, international students center, multicultural resource center, office of student life and services, office of student academic affairs, and services for students with disabilities. There should be lists of the cultural houses, cultural support groups, and organizations on campus.

It is also important to find those places that minority and low-income or first-generation college students might frequent. There may also be opportunities for collaboration with the agencies of diversity on campus and those that have programs for student learning and student support services. One librarian has a strong connection with some of the resident advisors (RAs) of residence halls. She finds it is an excellent way to let the RAs know that she is there to help. She also does library tables in the residence hall cafeterias and does some office hours in the residence hall libraries, always with some "tip sheets" and her contact information. She mentioned that the visibility is such a great promotional tool, and she fields a lot of reference questions that way as well.

Being visible also includes attending meetings related to diversity and making efforts to learn of events, issues, suggestions, and ways that you can help. Eventually, a goal would be to become a member or representative of campus organizations and committees such as the campus general education committee and campus diversity committee.

Community and National Relationships

Consider the stakeholders in the community and in state and national organizations that can be consulted. Attendance at conferences and participation in meetings held throughout the community and state can provide important networking opportunities. There are also efforts that can be made with students before they come to college. Those programs will be discussed in chapter 6.

Learn about Students' Cultures

This was a common goal of librarians. Because there are so many cultural groups on campus, it is important to learn how to best communicate and interact with those groups. Clearly, reading the literature and participating in training sessions conducted by individuals from specific cultural groups is an important task. Another method is to learn about students through conversations about what they know, believe, and value. Even though they cannot speak for everyone in their cultural or ethnic group, it is possible to hear common themes that will provide clues for working with others.

One interviewee remarked on lessons she learned when trying to gain an entrée with the Native American groups on campus:

> It could be challenging to know how to gain an entrée. I could see why someone would think, "I keep writing to those people and they never respond, and they never want to meet me." I could see where that could be disheartening if they think they're getting nowhere in the position and they think no one's responding the way they would imagine they would. I know now not to get offended by that. So, yea, getting those connections is difficult, especially if you don't know. You don't know that they're a little standoffish and you have to warm up. And I didn't know that until someone told me. And I thought, "Huh, that sounds familiar. That sounds like something that's happened with other groups." If you're not aware of some of the issues, even people working in the library a long time or the community; some people don't pay attention to stuff like that. They may not be thinking culturally why that's happening, but maybe only thinking along the lines of, "Yea they don't respond all that well." They don't think of maybe culturally why that's happening

Some ways to observe and learn about cultures while working with students:

- Observe how they use computers and resources and how they prefer to learn.
- Ask them questions that will help you gain some insight about their preferred communication and learning style. It is all right to ask if they prefer to know the process so they can repeat it later; if they prefer a hands-on approach or if they prefer to have you manipulate the keyboard; and if a handout would help.

- Try to observe if they prefer a direct or indirect style of communication.
- Observe how their nonverbal communication patterns differ from yours. Try to determine what they might be communicating to others. The same applies to intonation, tone, body stance, touch, and distance.

Once a librarian begins working with various populations, it becomes easier to ask questions and observe. It takes a while to build up trust and to be included into a community. It is fine to ask individuals if there is a more meaningful or helpful way to present or phrase something or how they interpret what was said. One librarian remarked, "You have to learn the social norms to be able to navigate or not be perceived as an interloper, you know, some horrible person. Sometimes you have to look into that and ask people, 'Is this o.k.?' If you don't know, you don't want to start out bad with a group just because you don't know socially what some of the norms were."

One of the most informative ways to hear what students think about library interactions is to invite a panel of students to respond to questions by librarians about their library experiences. Students from a similar culture might feel more inclined to open up, especially if the librarian who arranges the event has already built a level of trust with the students. Providing this type of forum for a group of librarians can be quite eye-opening if they hear students indicating how ineffective, judgmental, or threatening some experiences can be. On the other hand, students can share what has been most helpful and how they wish librarians would interact with them.

Gain an Entrée

Because so much of the job focuses on networking and relationships with individuals from other cultures, librarians were asked about challenges there. Gaining an entrée was one of the greatest challenges noted by the respondents. Engaging with individuals at the library, throughout the campus, and in the community requires good interpersonal skills. Finding the stakeholders is usually the first step in developing relationships. It may not be difficult to identify the relevant individuals in associations, cultural houses, academic support programs, learning support programs, disability services, or committees on campus, in the community, state, or nation. However, if these individuals are from cultures outside of one's own cultural group, there may be additional steps one might take. The next section outlines some ways to gain an entrée. It also provides some suggestions for becoming an ally.

Introductions

The importance of getting an introduction to the community was echoed in several interviews as a good way to begin the process of connecting with other communities. It may be a colleague, faculty member, student, staff person, or even a secretary that provides that first introduction. Having an introduction by someone from that community may help build the trust factor. Finding someone to provide an introduction to the desired group can be a very important consideration when approaching cultural groups outside of one's own. Not all individuals are as business-oriented or have the same interaction styles as others. Finding an individual who can vouch for you can help facilitate the process. There may be a student or staff or faculty member from that culture that can serve as a guide. A common expression by many of the interviewees was, "It's always helpful to have someone from the group bring you in." One librarian suggested, "I think that they need to make connections with those people who are diverse or underrepresented. And that's why it's helpful to have folks in the faculty who are diverse because when you have someone on the staff who is, then there is the interaction there. And that can be the interest of the folks that you want to connect to. That can save that mainstream person quite a bit of difficulties."

Sometimes it's the academic support staff that can provide that introduction. An African American librarian remarked, "They know the students and they might be the one person there day in and day out at the office so they really do know everyone. They might have the e-mail list or access to the people, [especially important] if there's been a lot of turnover. So it might be really important to build a connection with academic support staff. They are a great asset and definitely worthwhile to make sure that they are in your loop and a great advocate also."

Additionally, meeting someplace informal, as for coffee, can be a good way to ease into the conversation and to get to know a little about each other first. Various cultural groups like to develop rapport and get to know someone socially or chat a little before they discuss business or the task at hand. One can also begin to learn about expectations, socially accepted norms, and preference, which can begin the process of building trust. Once that connection is established, the librarian may proceed to ask how he or she can help the students or faculty in that department or area. The art of listening should definitely be encouraged. Rather than the librarian telling everything he or she would like to do, it is more important to listen to the areas of need and work together to come to an agreement of what might be done first, with an eye to other goals.

A librarian versed in Latino culture shared her experiences gaining an entrée to some of the constituencies on campus:

> You have to depend on the people who already work there and know the culture of the university. It would be horrible to get a position like this and not be able to have a supportive faculty member who you can work with and who can explain. Here's an example. I wrote to all my Native American faculty groups and I didn't get that enthusiastic of a response. And another librarian said, "Yea. We've noticed that that group, they are not as open." And I said, "Yea, I know that." I have a friend who is Navajo and I said, "It seems like those native groups are clicky" and she said, "Natives are clicky. You have to be brought into a group with natives." And she was Navajo and maybe she was just speaking from the perspective of Navajo perspective, but she came right out and said, "If you're not Native then it's hard to get into it because they're, you have to slowly work your way into there." And I thought, "Oh, that's a fantastic insight." If you think from your native view that that's how you need to work with one of these groups, well, o.k. That's like little things I've learned, and that I shouldn't take it personally or be offended that they're not as welcoming because culturally you kind of have to let them warm up to you a bit. And that's hard to know unless you know people and they talk to you and they're willing to talk to you about that.

Ask How You Can Help

During this chat it would be good to ask how you can help the students in their research needs. What would help facilitate learning for the students? You could also provide a few handouts and examples of ways that you could help with the research process, individual consultations, and program planning. Express interest in learning about specific programs, discussions, brown bags, presentations, and colloquia that you might be able to attend in order to get to know the community and the work being done by the faculty and students. This might also be a good opportunity to talk about collaboration and building a program together, including webpages, programming, instruction sessions, or workshops.

Become an Ally

One fallacy that numerous librarians mentioned was thinking that if a person is from an ethnic or cultural group outside of the mainstream culture that they will automatically know how to work with cultures other than their own. Each culture and group is distinct, and one needs to learn the nuances of any culture other than one's own. Someone from an underrepresented culture may be better able to understand some of the difficulties others may encounter in libraries if they have gone through that experience. However, ultimately they, too, may find themselves in situations outside of their comfort zone and will need to learn how to become allies with those other groups. One of the African American male librarians who was interviewed provided this suggestion about how to begin that process, for example, when discussing how a white mainstream librarian might be perceived:

> I think that at first the people might be a little standoffish and they're going to be looking at the person as "we don't really know where you're coming from and why are you doing this?" and I think you have to be persistent and I guess be true to your values. You know, if people think that you're doing it for the right reasons and that you're there to help them they will start to come to you and ask you questions and be willing to work with you. It's like you have to get a little foot hold and get somebody that you can work with and it starts to grow.

A female African American librarian offered, "First you need to be accepting and open-minded. When I say that, I think there are lots of different ways of doing things. People go with what they're most comfortable in doing and the others can be invisible. But the attention to those folks that are different will be invisible. Perhaps it's just a different way of doing the same thing and they need to be open-minded to that and be accepting."

A Latina librarian suggested:

> I think the important thing is listening to what they have to say and to try to understand. You have to first listen before you can understand. It's like when you meet someone who has an invisible disability, and they began to talk to you and you have to stop and listen to what they're saying, to be able to know how to help. It's similar to the reference interview or being a counselor. You have to listen to somebody and you have to be attentive and you have to respond and say "I hear you" or "I'm not sure I understand what I heard, can you repeat that" or "This is what I heard you say." I think taking on that kind of attitude perhaps helps, because then you're listening and you're trying to get the person to tell you what it is and how you need to respond.

An easy way to begin this process is to make yourself visible. Attend programs, colloquia, open forums, student presentations, celebrations, and talks. Show that you are interested in their work and culture. When librarians are visibly involved with students and faculty, they are more accepted as allies with a genuine interest in what that community is doing. Attendance at functions is also an excellent way to hear more about what the needs are and to make connections.

One librarian said, "I do believe you plant seeds and you keep watering to see what develops. If you start a workshop series this year, you revisit it next year to see if it was successful. People get used to seeing me at events and cultural centers. You just kind of are in the mix. And you then get people used to seeing you there and talking to them. When I was first in the position it was hard to do that, but now I'm able to do that."

The more visible the librarian is, in a friendly supportive role, the more comfortable others may be to later find the librarian and ask for assistance. There are opportunities, but it does take a little extra effort. Involvement on campus was an area that this librarian emphasized: "You have to kind of be involved with student groups. Always let them know you're there or around or you had this to offer and share a resource. We had people working with the ethnic youth for a long time but very few faculty knew, or even [staff] in our library. It was like, 'how are we working this if people don't even use the resources or know about the resources to recommend?' I think that whole awareness thing is definitely important."

Another example is from the author, who was previously the education reference librarian at a research library. She wanted to make a connection with the bilingual collegiate program (a support program mainly for Latinos) on campus because of her previous background working with Latinos and because she was fluent in Spanish. Previously that group had been rather neglected. She first got an introduction to the director of the program from her doctoral advisor, a Latina. From there she was introduced to the program, its staff, and the student groups and goals. She made herself available for research consultations, provided library help in their space, and worked with them on developing handouts, webpages, and joint programs. Eventually she created a one-credit bilingual course called "Essentials of Library Research" that all students in the program were encouraged to take. She became so engrained in their daily lives and successes and failures that she was invited to many graduations and celebrations, and even though she was a white Anglo American, she was accepted as an ally and "one of theirs." This outreach effort then extended to other minority support groups on campus.

The following, then, are some suggestions for becoming an ally:

- Show your interest in what others are doing. Make yourself visible by attending events and programs
- Be open-minded and flexible.
- Be genuine in your desire to get to know others and to learn about them and their efforts.
- Listen to others.
- Be attentive to how others prefer to communicate.
- Become involved.
- Be approachable and understanding.

Assess and Develop Appropriate Collections

Not everyone in these positions had collection development responsibilities. After a librarian resigned, at least two libraries took away that responsibility, thinking that would make the job easier. However, many librarians remarked that they felt that collection development needed to be part of the responsibility so that certain areas did not get overlooked. It also helped to build a connection with faculty in various areas because of the need to consult on collections related to ethnic or cultural groups. Even if a librarian has been hired without that duty, it is still possible to work with the collection development librarian to restructure the fund code to allow a code for selection of materials for underrepresented areas or to provide some funds for this effort.

Collection building for diverse populations has received a lot of attention in the past twenty years. There are already available many good resources to help build collections for various populations (see chapter 10). However, it is still important to work with areas on campus to ascertain that their needs are being met. Consulting with faculty regarding their research interests, student interests, and perceived gaps in the collection will help focus on some areas to investigate in collection building. Even a librarian who does not have collection development responsibilities can still gather suggestions for acquisitions and present them to the appropriate librarian in charge of collections. One suggestion was, "Look at the community that you're going to serve in and try to do some kind of needs assessment in terms of what kind of collection issues in programming that they need," and another librarian said it was important to "be open to knowing things and doing things differently. The collection is supposed to reflect the needs of your patrons." The message here was just because the library may not have collected in a certain area, style, genre, or topic, it does not mean that it cannot. If a particular group of users has need for something of a more popular nature or of an area not typically collected, that is an opportunity to bridge a gap.

One of the male African American librarians interviewed felt that collection development responsibilities should be an integral part of the job. However, with a limited budget, he has been pleased that many subject librarians have been picking up books related to various cultures and ethnic groups. That way, this librarian with limited funds is able to focus on what's falling through the gaps:

> For the most part, I wait till the end of the week before I go to the approval book room. So what I've been seeing over the years is that books that I normally would have had to purchase in my field are picked up by the other

selectors. So they're getting that part that we need to get a book on Native American literature and they should be purchasing a book rather than me. I can go look for more minute collections or the kind of history on native America or some other thing that's coming out that normally wouldn't come through our approval process. However, I don't think we're getting what we should be in terms of electronics though. Part of that may be the publishers that we normally work with are not putting out electronic material related to diverse cultures.

A librarian with responsibilities with Native American collections shared how her role in collection development interacts with other subject librarians: "I collect in certain departments but it's interdisciplinary. So for example, if I'm collecting in Native American studies I might get certain text. Actually, generally what I do is I pick up certain text that has not been picked up by other areas. The person who collects in history may very well collect text on Native American history, which leaves me free to pick up some of the more esoteric things that are not picked up by other departments."

Develop an Action Plan

As was mentioned earlier, an action plan is different from a plan of action. Whereas a plan of action is a way to help provide structure to tasks and to prioritize individual goals, an action plan looks more broadly at institutional goals and objectives. An action plan will help to put into perspective short- and long-range goals. Some librarians attempted to create one when they first arrived on the job, but soon realized they needed to know the culture of the library and campus a little before they could accomplish a plan. They needed to have developed contacts around campus who could partner in the efforts. Chapter 6 goes into further detail about creating an action plan, as well as a needs assessment.

Develop a Staff Training Program

Training librarians and staff to become culturally competent is a programmatic effort that requires the buy-in of library staff and administration, along with knowledge of individuals on campus and in the community who can participate. This topic will be further explored in chapter 7.

Develop and Offer Programs

Libraries are said to be the heart or "pulse" of the campus. In the past ten years, academic libraries have listened to their students as they asked for a more "homelike" environment, including comfortable seating, good lighting, a café, group and private study rooms, technology, and the many varied services of the campus combined into one place. For many, that has evolved into a learning or information commons. Many places also offer sections for gaming, for student presentations, brown bags, displays, and events. Additionally, libraries have partnered with campus and community groups to offer programming in the library, something previously thought to be a role of public libraries. There are many opportunities to develop programs that are inclusive. In fact, if one looks around the library, one should see materials that are representative of many cultures. Chapter 6 will provide some additional discussions about offering multicultural programming in libraries.

Summary

As discussed in chapter 2, librarians commented on having difficulty finding relevant examples of accomplishments, plans, and programs of multicultural or diversity librarians. They turned to various resources and people to learn what others were doing in similar positions. One librarian remarked, "When I was applying to this job I was looking for information about what people in these positions do and I couldn't find any. It got to the point that I asked my advisor from library school and asked 'could you put me into contact with people working in this area? I'm looking for good ideas of what they're doing.' That's how I sort of did my research in preparing for this job."

Over 30% of the librarians surveyed said they had difficulty finding examples of what to do as a diversity librarian. Many had collection development as one of their duties and may have had some library school preparation for that—but perhaps not for specific populations. They needed guidance on how to assess the collections and to work with their stakeholders in further developing a collection. They also wanted information on sequenced planning related to developing a diversity plan, mission statements, goals, objectives, action plans, training, and programming. They wanted to learn how to become culturally competent and to gain an entrée with their communities. One of those elements might be one person's full-time job, yet they were asked to do it all, plus instruction and reference. One goal would be to bring other librarians into the process to help spread the efforts throughout the institution. Yet it takes time to establish programs and training to even understand how others can become involved.

There are some excellent resources available to assist in these efforts, but one has to search extensively to find them. Many librarians had searched on the Web to find organizations, associations, and libraries involved with diversity efforts. They looked for examples of programming, training, collection development, and outreach. There are blogs, wikis, discussion groups, excellent articles, books, and training sessions available, if one has time to search. Unfortunately, there is not a good list of librarians working on these efforts. It is possible to find many "ethnic" librarians and Spectrum Scholars, but only a few of these might be serving in the role of "diversity librarian."

Finding information on individual library webpages was extremely difficult. One of the best ways for connecting with other librarians has been through diversity conferences, if one knows about them. Some regions of the country have developed diversity networks, such as California's Diversity in Academic Librarian's List (DIAL). DIAL, for example is a forum for librarians working with diverse populations. In addition to an e-mail discussion group, they have meetings. Chapter 10 provides some specific resources that might be consulted.

CHAPTER SIX

Organization and Management of Multicultural Services

Organizational culture, attitudes, and behaviors can have a major impact on efforts to promote diversity awareness and training. Negativity, resistance, and reluctance in these areas can not only impede progress, but can also lead to skilled and valued individuals looking for employment elsewhere. Many librarians in diversity positions felt at a loss for how to begin with organizing and managing multicultural services, especially if they were new to the field. They shared concerns about being able to "find a voice" and to "be recognized and respected for their work." They hoped to learn how to overcome barriers within the library related to achieving their goals and to garner support and involvement by other library personnel. The previous chapter provided some suggestions on how to get started in regards to establishing networks and outreach connections. This chapter will provide some models for establishing and managing multicultural services at libraries.

Assessing organizational culture is an important step to being able to articulate a clear mission (Kaarst-Brown et al., 2004). It also helps to facilitate organizational change. These also require library support with library leaders and managers trained in facilitating the change in organizational culture (Cameron and Quinn, 1999). It seems that many librarians in positions to help the library become a welcoming multicultural institution are left to figure it out on their own, rather than the library understanding that this individual is being asked, effectively, to change the culture of the organization without any leadership, support, or even awareness on the part of library administrators.

Assessing Organizational Culture
Organizational culture requires that groups establish ways to integrate individuals into the existing culture and also to adapt to the external

environment. A general definition of culture is provided by Edgar Schein (2004):

> The culture of a group can now be defined as: A pattern of shared basic assumptions that the group learned as it solved its problems of external adaptation and internal integration, that has worked well enough to be considered valid and therefore, to be taught to new members as the correct way to perceive, think, and feel in relation to those problems (p. 17).

When an individual enters an established culture and challenges the "correct way to perceive, think and feel," there can be resistance and possible backlash. Jameison and O'Mara (1991) observed that when an employee feels unwelcome and disrespected [in the workplace], an adversarial climate is created between the employee and management. As a result, job satisfaction and productivity become minimal at best, and the employee frequently quits. It is important to assess the culture to determine these basic assumptions before setting up a plan of action. It may be that an outside "change agent" can be consulted to help in the process, while evaluating the culture against the library's strategic goals. If diversity awareness, recruitment, and outreach are strategic goals, then the culture can be assessed to determine whether the assumptions, belief, and norms present help or impede the achievement of goals related to diversity. Schein (2004) provides some steps (below) that can be used to influence the culture of an organization:

Measure and control. Leaders can establish some level of expectation (measure) for participation in diversity programs, thus placing a recognizable importance in being involved. If individuals realize managers are looking to incorporate diversity efforts into the work flow, they may devote more effort to learning to be more culturally competent. Many of the librarians surveyed mentioned there was no measure, expectation, or accountability for librarians to participate in diversity efforts and training. Those institutions that mentioned success also mentioned the presence of certain mandates or requirements for participation. However, mandates without a clear message from administrators about the importance of these efforts may still lead to resentment if staff are required to participate without understanding why.

Leader reactions to critical incidents and organizational crises. An organizational crisis or critical incident provides an opportunity to reassess values, beliefs, and subsequent actions. Change may follow if leaders are careful with the approach they take after a crisis or critical incident. There may be a number of issues related to diversity either internal to the library or at the campus or national levels that can be used as exemplars of why it is important to reassess values.

Deliberate role modeling, teaching, and coaching. If managers and administrators play a role in promoting and advocating for diversity training, inclusion, recruitment, and outreach, they can set an example to the rest of the library staff of the importance and value of these efforts.

Criteria for allocation of rewards and status. A great motivator for participation is providing rewards for being willing to step outside of one's comfort zone and become involved in various diversity efforts. Leaders can effectively change organizational climate by advancing, retaining, and recruiting individuals with desirable values. Conversely, that also means that those not holding those values will be left behind.

Organizational design and structure. This process looks at the basic structure of the organization to determine, for example, if a different alignment will facilitate better communication. It would prove advantageous to the diversity librarian to be able to communicate vertically and horizontally. Design and structure may also involve looking at how units, departments, and committees are aligned as well.

Organizational systems and procedures. A newcomer to an organization can observe with fresh eyes how things are done and begin to question whether those ways are effective or not. However, making suggestions for change may not be well received if others do not want their way of doing things challenged. Having good communication strategies is imperative if one wants to suggest alternate approaches that break with tradition.

Stories about important events and people. Libraries are ideal places to provide examples of important events and people. Librarians can collaborate with leaders of the community from different cultures and diversities to speak with librarians about their culture. They can emphasize the importance of including stories, images, and examples from many cultures in the library's webpages, user guides, bibliographies, instruction sessions, exhibits, posters, displays, and events. Including members from diverse cultures in planning, training, and programming not only promotes diversity, but also indicates that it is important and valued.

Formal statements of organizational philosophy, creeds, and charts. Leaders need to see if diversity is included in the mission, value statements, and strategic plans. However, providing them in print is only the first step. Action steps and measurable outcomes need to be in place in order to assess progress and to gauge the effect of the efforts on the culture of the organization.

Ideally, assessing the organizational culture is a task that should involve not only the administration but also the staff. For the diversity librarian, the above might be used as talking points with the administration and with others to get the pulse of the organizational culture and the areas where one might be able to suggest changes.

Suggestions for Getting Buy-In

Unfortunately, typical comments voiced by librarians in these positions were that the organizational culture did not seem too flexible, that other librarians felt threatened by the presence of a librarian concerned with diversity efforts, or that librarians and staff did not fully understand why a diversity librarian was hired. Without the library leaders framing the importance of changing the culture to be more inclusive, diversity librarians have little hope of making advances. Following are some tips that might help get buy-in among library staff members.

Tell your story. One of the first things one librarian did was to ask to hold a public forum to introduce herself to everyone. In that capacity, she "shared her heart" with them about why she felt the work of promoting diversity was so important and how she hoped each one would be open to helping her think of ways to improve the library experience for others.

Acknowledge a need for help. It was clear from this study and also from speaking with numerous diversity librarians at conferences that they needed help in areas such as identifying the scope and responsibilities of the job, identifying priorities, initiating programs, and recruiting individuals to help with projects. Itemizing a list of all the areas of need is a first step toward finding individuals to help fill those slots. This also sends the message that the diversity librarian serves more as a coordinator of efforts and catalyst for change, rather than as the sole agent of change.

Listen to the stories of others. Another librarian set up coffee breaks with librarians and staff members who were suggested to her as interested in diversity initiatives. She listened to their stories of struggles and successes and noted their suggestions for improvements.

Recruit individuals who have already been active in promoting diversity. Although this may seem like an obvious statement, it is important to acknowledge the past work of these individuals so they feel valued for the work they have done. They may be key individuals for helping in future efforts. Turning to them for guidance and suggestions may also empower them and help create pride in what they can contribute.

Make allies of the reluctant ones. No doubt there are individuals who are reluctant to learn something outside of their comfort zone. It is usually easy to identify these individuals through daily encounters or by word of mouth. They may feel comfortable with the way things have been done and feel inconvenienced if asked to consider other approaches, protocols, training, or programming. They may be the ones that will grumble to others about efforts being made to the exclusion of something else. Perhaps they feel threatened, insecure, inadequate or perhaps even wronged. Rather than ignoring the situation, take time to understand the reluctance of these individuals. Listening to their stories is extremely important. There must be some reason they are putting up a barrier. After one librarian witnessed some hostility to a programming idea, she asked the librarian if they could talk. She asked if she had done something wrong and if there was something the other person could help her with to make the situation better. The other librarian was startled that she was being asked for help. Not knowing how to respond, she said, "No, it's not that you're doing anything wrong, it's just that I was never given the opportunity to develop any programming before and I guess I'm just feeling bitter about it." Rather than get defensive, the diversity librarian said she was thrilled that there was someone else with an interest in programming because she really needed someone with some great ideas to help her out. What the diversity librarian did was to acknowledge her own shortcomings and recognize a potential strength of the other librarian. She was able to recruit her to work on programming with her. That simple conversation made an ally out of the reluctant librarian. There are numerous other ways to find out why someone is reluctant and to find something they are good at that has been overlooked. By recognizing strengths of others they may be more inclined to use that strength to help out.

On the other hand, there may be some librarians who are uncomfortable with the whole idea of diversity awareness and training. Having conversations with them is also very important, although the real reasons may not surface. Instead, finding commonalities (either personal or work-related) with them can be a first step to beginning a relationship and establishing common goals, whether it is to provide the most welcoming reference service, creating webpages that are representative of all cultures, or developing better liaison services.

Diversity Assessment

While evaluating the organizational culture, certain patterns related to how open and supportive the library and staff are with diversity issues may surface. Doing an environmental scan related to diversity can help determine priorities for action.

The following questions, adapted from Glaviano and Lam (1990) and used in a self study by Love (2001), can help provide initial feedback of areas related to diversity within an organization.

1. How are we doing as colleagues and co-workers in developing positive working relationships?
2. Are there policies and procedures in place to ensure long term effectiveness of diversity initiatives?
3. How well are we serving our diverse populations that make up our user groups?
4. What can we do better to facilitate services?
5. Are our communication processes supportive at all personnel levels within the academic library?
6. Is the library environment inviting to all constituents of the university community?
7. Have we identified the benefits of diversity and know how to utilize them within our organization? (p. 77)

Data Gathering to Determine Strengths, Weaknesses, Opportunities, and Threats

It may be that answers to the above questions are not immediately apparent. Developing assessments can help to better gauge strengths and weaknesses in these areas. Ideally a professional library consultant would be hired to assist with the assessment. At minimum it will require the support of the administration, help from the diversity committee, and assistance with analyzing the data. The assessments can be both qualitative and quantitative, depending on what is being measured. Depending on resources and time, a variety of data gathering methods can be used. Following are some examples.

SWOT Analysis (Strengths, Weaknesses, Opportunities, and Threats)
The SWOT analysis is a method to analyze the strengths, weaknesses, opportunities and threats to an institution related to various issues, dynamics, and trends. Once the strengths and assets, as well as the gaps and weaknesses are identified, plans can proceed to address the most urgent needs regarding diversity and equity. Because it concentrates on the issues that potentially have the most impact, the SWOT analysis is useful when a very limited amount of time is available. Some examples of areas related to diversity that could be analyzed with this method include staff, facilities, technology, resources, collection, supporters, organizational structure, and current products and services.

Quantitative Methods
- Demographic data. Statistical data should be available on campus that detail student enrollment by ethnicity, race, foreign population, and those registered with the office of disabilities and learning disabilities
- Surveys. Surveys can be useful in gathering a broad response. They can be designed with only a few questions and given to individuals at service points in the library or to faculty to give to their students at the end of a class. They can also be longer. Surveys could be developed for faculty, students, and library staff to assess different dimensions and distributed via the Web.

Qualitative Methods
- Interviews. There are various types of interviews that can be conducted. Interviews allow the gathering of more detailed information and examples and stories. It is important to spend time listening to the participants and asking follow-up questions. It may be that your prepared questions do not get covered in the time allotted, but you may come away with very revealing information if you listen carefully to what the interviewee says and probe for a bit more. It is important not to make judgments or assumptions, but to begin by developing some rapport. It may be hard to open up to a stranger and reveal fears, anxieties, or unsuccessful interactions, so take some time to chat informally, which may help break the ice. Conducting a two- or three-part interview may allow for better rapport.

- Focus Groups. Focus groups can be very informative in hearing the perspectives of a small (six to twelve) group of individuals on a given topic. Oftentimes a comment from one individual will spark an example or contribution by another individual. These are best facilitated by someone from outside the library who can be neutral in directing the questions.
- Observation and Participation. By observing interaction between individuals in a natural setting, it may be possible to get a more realistic example of cultural norms and practices. Attendance and participation at meetings, conferences, cultural gatherings, programs, and lectures are some ways of learning more about individuals.

Regardless of the type of data-gathering tool, good preparation of questions, scripts, and protocols is important. It is always a good idea to have others review the questions first to help with phrasing and to catch possible bias and leading questions. For some guidelines for conducting interviews see Alire and Archibeque (1998), Gupta (1999), and Seidman (2006). When doing assessments, it is important to respect the cultural mores of groups and include the targeted participants in the planning and execution of the assessments. Also include them in the data analysis to get their impressions of the findings and perhaps to help set priorities for an action plan.

Diversity Committees

One of the best mechanisms for a librarian who coordinates diversity efforts is to have a diversity committee. Many libraries do have some sort of committee or working group to at least plan diversity events, exhibits, education, and training, even if there isn't a designated librarian for diversity efforts. If such a committee does not exist, that might be one of the first things to create. The diversity committee can serve as a sounding board for ideas and help to establish connections and initiate efforts. The committee can be comprised of faculty, staff, and students from the community. The presence of a diversity committee can be a signal to others that the library is interested in being an inclusive environment.

Developing a Diversity Plan of Action

Although many of the librarians in this study commented about the organizational culture of their library and also the need to do surveys and studies related to diversity efforts, none of them had done a formal assessment to determine priorities and first steps. Most had a sense of what they wanted to accomplish related to diversity but had not developed a plan of action. They worked to establish relationships across campus, developed diversity committees, and begun diversity training and programs. Many also recognized the importance of contributing or creating the following:

- definition of diversity
- development of a shared vision
- mission statement
- diversity committee
- diversity training program
- diversity action plan
- assessment plan

However, much of the above was done as opportunities arose, rather than as a result of a sequenced plan. Developing an action plan provides a framework for work to be done, not only by the diversity librarian, but by others. It includes a timeline, documentation of resources needed, goals, and assessment.

Diversity committees are most likely the groups that will help create an action plan for diversity efforts. After assessing the climate and getting background information, the committee may first draft a working paper that provides the background for the work to be done. An example of this process was done at the University of Massachusetts Amherst campus (Mestre et al., 1997). The Diversity Working Group that created this plan also advised on making diversity visible in the vision and mission statements and in the strategic plan that was developed. They also contributed to a diversity action plan (University of Massachusetts Amherst Libraries, 2005).

Developing an action plan should be tied to the library's strategic plan, mission and vision statement, if they exist. Western Michigan University (Potter et al., 2006) developed an excellent action plan with guides and a tracking template for developing an action plan. The goals that they developed are

1. To develop and maintain a shared and inclusive understanding of diversity, multiculturalism, institutional bias, and affirmative action through training and education at every level of the institution.
2. To investigate and put into place an institutional infrastructure that dismantles institutional bias, and

recognizes, supports, and sustains the efforts of this diversity
and multiculturalism initiative at all levels of the institution.

3. To create a welcoming and inclusive university environment
(climate) that includes recursive training, curriculum reform,
and research incentives.

4. To recruit, retain, and graduate a diverse student body and
promote a diverse workforce at all levels.

5. To enhance curricular, co-curricular, research, service,
independent, creative, artistic, and study abroad activities
as a means to fully engage the university community in an
affirming diverse and multicultural learning environment
as well as include curriculum development and pedagogical
strategies that address the needs and interests of the changing
student population.

6. To develop and maintain consistent accountability measures
in order to accurately assess progress towards institutionalizing
diversity and multiculturalism (at all levels) on an annual
basis. (p. 12)

The action steps included in the plan provide a framework with priorities of what the next steps are in each goal. See chapter 10 for resources
related to this.

Academic Program Development

There are usually some programs already in place at libraries to assist different populations to take advantage of library services.

These programs may have been established through instructional
or outreach services or may be established at the university. The library
should be included in their programs with at least a workshop at the library to introduce these constituencies them to the ways the library will
be able to help them in their studies (both currently and in the future).
Webpages and user guides can be created so that any number of librarians
can participate in these programs. Below are some examples of minority
programs on campuses:

Pre-college programs. These programs are geared for middle and high
school students and are designed to encourage college enrollment and, in
some cases, science majors. Such programs include Howard Hughes Life
Sciences Programs, high school summer science training programs, and
Upward Bound. Students often come to campus during the summer to

be part of the college experience. Introducing them to the library should be part of the program.

Bridging programs. These programs are designed to assist in both academic and social transition from high school to college. Examples include Upward Bound, the Alliances for Minority Participation (AMPS), and other transition programs that work primarily with low-income or first-generation students.

Undergraduate programs. There are several programs designed to inspire minority undergraduates to pursue advanced studies, and librarians can have a much more integrated role with these projects. Some of these programs are the Mellon Minority Undergraduate Program, the Minority Engineering Program, the Ronald E. McNair Scholars programs, and the Summer Research Opportunity Program (SROP) at Big 10 universities. Universities may also have their own programs.

Student Support Services and Resource Centers on Campus. These may also be provided in cultural houses or centers. Librarians can offer support, drop-in hours, and workshops; help to build collections in the center; and offer to cosponsor programs, workshops, and classes.

Minority Faculty Development Programs. Although not as common as other programs, this type of program can include library components to assist in educating faculty in effectively using the library's resources.

Library Outreach Programs

There are many ways to get out and connect with students. Because students may be reluctant to visit the library or to ask for help, the diversity librarian and others need to think of other ways of providing assistance.

Following are some examples of providing library outreach:

- Be a presence in the dorms: provide flyers to post, connect with the resident assistants, ask to be on the agenda for residence hall meetings, and especially create a presence in the residence hall libraries. Periodically set up a resource table in the residence hall cafeterias.
- Connect with the student support services and the cultural houses on campus and offer regular library hours in house. Work with students to create user guides with clear and easy-to-follow instructions and programs targeted to their needs.
- Offer to be a guest speaker at student association meetings.

- Contribute a column such as "Library News, or "Library Tips" to the student newspapers, departmental newsletters, flyers, blogs, and webpages.
- Provide a table at various locations on campus at the beginning of each semester.
- Cosponsor workshops with the job fairs; technology fairs; counseling groups; and admission, scholarship, and financial aid offices.
- Offer special library workshops that can be conducted in small or large groups. Try to arrange like-participants for workshops, such as a special workshop for ESL students, or by topic. Try to avoid packaging too much content into the workshop, but emphasize that they can contact you for one-to-one research help.
- Take time to listen to the students' needs and include their ideas about improving library service programs as part of the library planning decision-making process.

Recognizing Accomplishments

It takes many dedicated individuals to help a library become more welcoming and inclusive. Much of the work may even be done behind the scenes. It is important to let others know what is being done at the library and who is contributing to the efforts. By publicizing the efforts, innovative ideas, and advances, others see that the library is committed to fostering an environment that embraces all.

The Library Diversity Committee at the University of Michigan (www.lib.umich.edu/library-diversity-committee/about-us) annually recognized an individual or group who had made a significant contribution to the library's diversity program with the Annual Diversity Award. The award was presented at the Annual Library Diversity Celebration. The award recipient received a gift certificate, and recipients' names were added to the Diversity Award plaque, which resides in the second floor lobby of the Graduate Library.

Assessment

Assessment of progress related to diversity is challenging because some goals and actions are not easily quantifiable. Few academic libraries have published their diversity assessment plans, which makes it difficult to look at models and examples. However, Love (2001) developed an instrument that looked at shifting power dynamics, diversity of opinion, lack of empathy, tokenism, participation, and overcoming inertia, which areas were adapted from a Joplin and Daus (1997). Love also included awareness of diversity issues, learning, and racism as other variables to be included in the assessment.

Progress towards broad diversity and multiculturalism goals could also be assessed by

- positive changes in student, faculty, staff, and administrator perceptions of the climate and their experiences
- increased diversity in the composition of the librarians, staff, and administrator populations as well as the multicultural programs, services, policies, practices, and outreach efforts
- positive institutional changes to the decision-making processes, personnel, budget, and plans put in place to address the needs and interests of all those recruited.

Various librarians have administered other diversity assessment instruments such as that done by the library diversity committee at the University of Tennessee (Royse, Conner, & Miller, 2006). The committee used a survey to assess the climate of the library prior to beginning their diversity efforts. Diversity forums and conferences often have programs from individual libraries regarding their assessment efforts.

Summary

A change in organizational culture often occurs when one attempts to bring social justice education and diversity awareness to an organization. Working to change the culture of an organization is an effort that needs to be integrated throughout the library beginning with direction by the administration. A lot of ground work needs to occur before a librarian can begin efforts in helping staff become culturally competent. Assessing the culture, bringing in stakeholders, creating working groups, developing a rapport with others, and developing a mission statement, goals, and action plan will assist in providing the support and foundation needed to proceed with initiatives.

CHAPTER SEVEN

Staff Training and Library Orientation Programs

P roviding diversity education opportunities for all future and current librarians is becoming more critical than ever as our society becomes more diverse. Libraries have a variety of ways they try to address the need for diversity training, such as hiring a librarian, establishing diversity committees to coordinate efforts, or sending librarians to diversity workshops or conferences. Educating all librarians to become culturally competent should be the goal of both library schools and libraries. If this type of education occurred in library schools, then the diversity librarian could continue with ongoing training and programmatic opportunities. Chapter 8 pertains more specifically to suggestions for library schools. Until such time that all librarians leave library school with foundational knowledge related to diversity and cultural competency, libraries will still need to find ways to bridge this gap with on-the-job training. This chapter will provide some suggestions for ways to provide diversity training and awareness at libraries.

Even if a library has been fortunate enough to hire a designated librarian for diversity efforts, to expect one librarian to be solely responsible for educating all others can be a daunting task, especially with everything else the person has to do. Becoming culturally competent is a long process. It takes time to reflect, absorb, and then integrate the information. An important element for success in library-wide training is the support of the administration. If the coordinator provides training opportunities without support from the administration (including mandated training), the result may be low attendance and an inability to achieve the desired outcomes. Following are some of the issues related to diversity training shared by librarians in this study.

Some Issues Related to Diversity Training
Reluctance to Engage in Diversity Efforts
It is rare to find an institution that has been able to infuse diversity training and cultural awareness and sensitivity into the mindset of staff.

Librarians encountered several challenges in their diversity training efforts. The first challenge seemed to be reluctance of staff to attend training. Librarians reported that oftentimes few individuals participated in available training and programs. Some of this may be due to a lack of accountability or expectation for staff to participate. Specific comments shared included these:

- "Many staff members have been in place for several years. There is somewhat of an environment of hesitation to try something new."
- "Developing a common understanding of goals, approaches and even vision is difficult."
- " There is a lack of initiative among senior staff."
- "Politics seems to be an ever present shadow."

Some of the reluctance to engage in diversity training might stem from individuals feeling they will be held accountable for negative progress or interactions. They might also resent that they are being asked to change their current practices. Some researchers attribute this reluctance to a lack of positive organizational effects (Arai, Wanca-Thibault, & Shockley-Zalabak, 2001; Bendick, Egan, & Lofhjelm, 2001; Holladay et al., 2003).

It is important to remember that employees are at different stages of diversity development, so connecting to each one on their specific concerns, needs and interests can help to develop a rapport and to begin to earn their trust.

Library Support

Overcoming politics is a challenge that really needs to be addressed at the administrative level. The administration needs to clearly state the value and importance of participation in these efforts. Administrators also need to be clear about expectations and desired outcomes. This message needs to be repeated continually, rather than stated just once and then assuming uniform buy-in. Without library support, employees may feel as though they are being forced to attend these training workshops. They first need to understand the foundational needs and values of racial equality and becoming culturally competent. Howland (2001, p. 111) noted, "Employees who are required to attend diversity training against their will, and who already hold negative attitudes and stereotypes about other groups, are likely to become even more negative, rather than more positive and accepting."

Motivating Individuals

In recent years there has been a shift from affirmative action to broader diversity issues. It is important for all staff to know their role in providing a welcoming environment for every person who uses the library's services—whether in person, by phone, by or e-mail, letter, or instant message (chat).

Joplin and Daus (1997, p. 41) suggest that librarians should "listen, with empathy, in a way that inspires openness and trust, while attempting to understand where others are coming from, what they have been through, and where they are going." This piece of advice works well in almost any situation. Once individuals feel they have been heard, they may feel more validated and can step back to hear what others have to say.

When librarians are open to engaging in a dialogue or are willing to try something new, it then becomes a matter of finding an area that they feel is one of their strengths. In fact, it could be as simple as adding a few representative cultural examples in their subject guide or webpage for a particular class. Taking small steps at the beginning and experiencing success at those levels (and no repercussions) is a gentle way to begin infusing diversity throughout the fabric of the institution. Clearly there are many other steps needed, but getting other librarians to understand the efforts they can make in the process is a critical step.

Diversity Training Programs

Diversity programs are characteristic of many organizations committed to providing employees with a "tool kit" to help individuals develop an understanding of cross-cultural communication skills, disability awareness, and cultural sensitivity. They can also help individuals to adjust their frame of reference to match those that are being served. Diversity training and mentoring programs can help provoke individual changes. This is an area that takes great energy. A sequenced plan of training might be established by the diversity committee. However, unless the training is mandatory, it may reach only those who are already interested in these issues and not the individuals who need it the most. One librarian in the study shared her experience with mandating training:

> [When we first did these programs] these were mandatory for the staff to attend at that point. The dean at that point was saying it was mandatory, although no

one checked. It got to a point where we did well with no one to mandate this. We wanted to encourage them to attend and go back and discuss it in the unit. We had lots of folks outside the library coming in too, because it was open to the campus as well. In the latter years, that changed and it wasn't mandatory and you couldn't get the attendance.

The above comment is representative of similar feedback from other librarians of the importance of requiring diversity training. Although there may initially be resistance if training is required, if the training is done well it will become something that people look forward to attending. Follow-up should also be incorporated into the training program. Without the attendance requirement, individuals may find excuses not to participate. The diversity committee could decide how it will make individuals accountable, or perhaps the administration might reward individuals based on their accounting of individual's efforts with diversity advancement in their annual review.

Suggestions for Beginning a Diversity Training Program
Obtain Library Support
For any diversity initiative to succeed, leadership must provide a commitment to the process. Diversity training and cross-cultural awareness fit very well with library missions and professional practices. One librarian in the study shared her process for planning programs:

When I begin a program I have a full understanding from the inside before going to someone outside. So as we were doing planning for the program we would plan a year ahead in the committee meetings. We planned our program and came to consensus about the program and who to invite. And when I went outside the library to get help to do the programming there was less resistance to participate. It got to a point that most of them were like, "Okay that sounds great, what would you like me to do? You tell me what you want me to do. Who would like me to speak to?" So it got to a point that I knew who to go to for soliciting participants or speakers. At least in my experience, I need to craft what this program is going to be about, what it is going to cover and how we are going to cover it and then to get faculty and staff to please come and speak to this.

It would be difficult to go out and try to reach people when you aren't sure about how well they'll be accepted in the library once they get there. I can't imagine doing that without support. It's like going out and pulling people into your house and you have no clue what's in your house. You would need the inside support to know what you can do and can't do and who you are going to invite in.

The library administration needs to be the driver behind diversity efforts so that staff understand the importance and will take an active role in initiatives and training. Ongoing involvement and participation by the management in training and advocacy can demonstrate the importance of projects for all staff and job families. Getting library support may include bringing in outside speakers to emphasize the importance of library diversity efforts or creating a white paper regarding diversity issues and goals. Winston's edited book (1999) presents relevant diversity issues for administrators to consider. It includes definitions, a rationale for promoting diversity, and the importance of clarifying diversity goals and priorities to be achieved. It also provides suggested approaches to accomplish diversity inclusiveness.

Research Best Practices

There are many books, articles, and websites available that provide diversity training examples. Dewey and Parham (2006), for example, edited a volume that includes chapters with suggestions and advice on how to create a diversity plan, how to recruit and retain a diverse workforce, and how to improve diversity through services, collections, and collaborations. Neely and Lee-Smeltzer (2002) compiled selected papers that illustrate ways libraries can work toward diversity integration in academic libraries. The ALA (2008) Office for Diversity provides a clearinghouse for diversity resources. It provides resources on diversity issues including creating a diversity action and inclusion plan, diversity climate surveys, recruitment, and retention and training. The Houston Area Library System (2004) developed some online training modules to help facilitate customer service for diverse populations, including suggestions for cross-cultural communication. The Colorado Department of Education (2008a, 2008b) provides numerous resources related to creating a diversity plan, engaging staff (training), creating programs, and identifying leaders in library diversity. There are also resources that serve to compile diversity best practices and suggestions. One such resource is the Ocean County Library's Diversity Database (2007), which gathers diversity programs. The database is browsable and searchable by community, age group, and difficulty. Others can contribute programs to the database as well. Another online resource that includes a lot of workshops and examples for staff training is Web Junction (2008). Currently there are sections devoted to people with disabilities, immigrants and world languages, Spanish speakers, and tribal and First Nation communities. Other representative resources are included in Chapter 10.

Identify Partners

Identify the agencies, groups, or individuals in your community with whom you might partner for training or tap as consultants or facilitators. Many campuses have a training and development center. Also worth investigating is the social justice education program, disability services, learning disabilities groups, student affairs, academic affairs, ethnic media, ethnic organizations on campus, community services organizations and associations, library schools, public schools, and other colleges and universities in the area for individuals with special knowledge or experience in diversity training. If on campus, these individuals will most likely provide these training sessions without fee. Several individuals in the study provided specific concerns related to the need for embracing diversity or establishing relationships.

- "I think getting the library (staff and Admin) to keep a focus on diversity in the current climate of retracking on Affirmative Action is critical."
- "I coordinate the Latino Services Network group of local agencies that provide services to Latinos. It takes a lot of time to coordinate this and although everyone has good intentions, we still step on toes and overlap services sometimes and have difficulty communicating. We're working on it, though, and I feel it's one of the most important things I do."

Conduct a Needs Assessment

There are several types of needs assessments that might be used to help develop a diversity training program. One is a campus community assessment to determine the demographics and needs of targeted campus communities related to diversity efforts. Another is of the library's diversity climate, which will help to gauge readiness for and attitudes toward diversity training. An example of this type of assessment is provided by Royse (2006). Her survey assessed the readiness of librarians to develop a diversity program. Yet another is to specifically assess the type of diversity training to be done at the library, which can help find gaps that need to be addressed. A pre- and post-training assessment can be beneficial in order to provide benchmarks. The needs assessment can help determine how much training is needed and to prioritize topics to address and helps begin the process of inclusion by asking for input related to diversity from staff and the community.

There are various options for providing assessments. One method for staff training is to provide a self-assessment. Self-assessments allow participants to examine their own cultural beliefs and behaviors, which may help them to realize the areas that they might need to focus on for improvement. They then may be more receptive to activities and debriefings that illustrate how these perceptions influence their approaches to cross-cultural communication and interactions (Brown, 2006; Banks, 2001; Zeilchner and Hoeft, 1996). Brown (2006) also provides a strategy for helping individuals examine their cultural heritage in order raise self-awareness and to improve cross cultural knowledge and interaction.

Assessments should be conducted and distributed at opportune times throughout the year or before or after training programs. Diversity assessment needs to be ongoing and part of the larger library strategic initiatives in order to assure it is given adequate emphasis (Black, 2002). Hubbard (2003) also provides some relevant suggestions and tools for measuring diversity initiatives. Chapter 10 provides some specific resources for assessment.

After the Needs Assessment: Next Steps

The results of the needs assessment should provide valuable information to determine the types of training that would be useful, both short- and long-term. Following are some steps and suggestions for moving past the assessment stage.

Develop Objectives

Based on the needs assessment, decide what the focus of the training will be. The focus should be narrow enough to be able to cover that targeted area and not be overwhelming. It may be necessary to split the training into a few different sessions, one held each month, to give time for reflection and follow-up work between the sessions. For example, it may be determined that cross-cultural communication, assisting students with learning disabilities, learning styles, or interpreting nonverbal communication are identified as areas of importance. Even though there may be many other areas that surface as gaps in knowledge or comfort level, tackling one at a time in a sequenced approach may help individuals to devote the necessary mental and emotional resources to absorb the information of the training sessions. If there is a diversity committee, it can assist in developing a plan for training and to connect with partners to secure facilitators, to develop pre- and post-assessments, and to perform any other assignments.

Design Informational and Transformational Programs

Because individuals learn in multiple ways, it is important to provide multiple modes of learning. Some individuals may also be uncomfortable with group work or active learning exercises (so often useful in training sessions). Therefore, it is helpful to provide multiple types of programs to help meet the needs of multiple participants. Initially, informational programs may be necessary to introduce some of the concepts. An example of informational programs would be communicating the mission, policies, procedures, and service ethic of the library to new employees. Those sessions can be short or even done through videos or PowerPoint presentations available on the Web so that employees can view them at any time. Adding some review elements through self-check quizzes can help reinforce some of the points made.

Once the basics are covered, training can progress to transformational programs. Transformational programs are those that provide opportunities for employees to develop their cross-cultural skills, attitudes, or beliefs. An example of a transformational program would be panel discussions at the library consisting of students from the various ethnic and cultural groups, as well as from learning and disability services. An example provided by one of the study participants follows:

> One thing we did last year was a recent panel of students
> from diverse panels to come and speak with staff about what

their experience at the library has been, what they hope the library would offer or why they don't use the library, which was really eye-opening, I think for staff. That is something that I'm going to try to do again this year and also to bring in some more formal speakers. And I would like to bring in some speakers across campus who are working with various elements of working with diverse cultures to help staff and explain to them how they are working with people across campus. That's one way we're trying to make the later committed to reaching out to students and having it go both ways. Reaching out and then having them tell us what they want, so that we can do our jobs better.

It can be very difficult for the diversity librarian to be the person talking to the staff. It is very different to have the representatives of the various cultures come in and talk, because that yields an air of authenticity and reality about the situations, circumstances, and experiences of the targeted group. The fact that someone internal to the library has advanced degrees or is considered an expert in the field may become invisible to library staff. There is oftentimes more attention and credence given to outside speakers. Bringing in the people affected by library services and hearing their stories and experiences can make an impact.

Use Various Methods and Media
If the focus of the training is skills, then one might use role-playing, communication exercises, storytelling, videos, simulations, vignettes, and so forth. Short readings, self-assessments, or presentations by expert guest speakers are good tools for building knowledge and awareness. If the focus of the training is on attitudes and beliefs, one might bring in outside facilitators or panelists from a particular cultural group to lead the group through exercises and discussions. Not everyone is comfortable with active learning exercises. It may be helpful to solicit some individuals ahead of time who would be willing to assist in role-playing or simulation exercises in case the audience is somewhat reluctant to volunteer.

Assess the Effectiveness of the Training
In addition to providing a sequenced training program and possibly making it mandatory, there needs to be some sort of reflection as a result of

the program. Follow-up evaluations and assessments to determine how the library was progressing was not a common practice among librarians surveyed, except for indicating the programs that were offered and how many people attended. Rather than people attending the program and not engaging further with the information, some sort of action should be built into the training program. To begin with, a short assessment of participants' knowledge and cultural awareness before and after training sessions to determine if the objectives are met could be done. Following are some examples of activities to assign the participants.

- List three ways that you might change what you do based on today's training session.
- Over coffee or lunch, share the highlights of what you gained from this session with at least one other person.
- Revise a document, webpage, or procedure to incorporate the information you gained from this session
- Offer a specific diversity program relevant to your own library department that will offer suggestions for modifying efforts of the department to better accommodate individuals.

Realize That Training Is a Long-Term Process

Cross-cultural awareness does not happen in one session, so training should be viewed as an ongoing, integral part of orientation and continuing education in the library. A reflection from one librarian in the study reiterated that point:

> Even when people have had cross cultural communication or sensitivity training it's still very hard and intimidating for people who come from a background where they don't have a lot of exposure to different groups. That's scary in itself. It can still be intimidating and in a situation where it comes up you don't immediately think of that. It's not ingrained. All the training in the world won't make it an ingrained response. At least, you have to be dedicated to it. It can't be a once a year workshop, it needs to be every day where it becomes an inherent response, rather than "Oh, I remember they told us about that in training." It has to be more than a training that's an optional thing that people can come to. And the next year they'll do something different.

Share the Responsibility

The best scenario would be to have all librarians working together to develop various aspects of training and program development. Until individuals have developed the rapport and shared vision of working collegially, there may still be tensions. When approached individually to think about ways of becoming more inclusive, librarians may become defensive at first. One librarian in the study became hesitant to suggest ways to increase diversity in the libraries (with collections or even with bulletin boards) with certain individuals because "when you start to do that people start to get real defensive and think that you are accusing them of being racist."

It is important to establish the need for collaborative relationships when working with collections and services. If individuals haven't been through diversity training, they may not be looking holistically at the collection or at how it is or isn't serving various populations. They may be viewing the collection only from their perspective. This individual type of training is much more challenging because it is dealing with real, concrete issues that affect services. Establishing a shared goal and determining how each person can contribute to achieve the outcome should be a shared desire.

An example of this in action was described by one African American librarian in the study:

> When I started here there was still a lot of buzz around AIDS and how it was affecting the community and so we had a meeting with the science librarian, the medical librarian, the social work librarian, and the graduate library on who would collect what on AIDS. The medical librarian would collect strictly medical stuff. They were going to look at prognosis and the whole medical end of how you treat the thing. Social work was like "we're only into the social aspect" and then there's the whole public health. We had to sit down and try to figure who would collect what, what journals and that started like a collaborative process among all the libraries which made it easier for me than to go over and talk about a lot of stuff.

Make Diversity Visible

An easy and important way to work towards creating an inclusive environment is to make diversity visible in user guides, webpages, posters, bulletin boards, and handouts. By integrating images, citations, and excerpts from individuals of various cultures, the library is indicating that it values diversity, as well as the contributions and efforts made by individuals from all cultures. For example, there are many ways to augment guides to include diversity, such as providing links to examples of multicultural resources, including images, and highlighting citations from various individuals throughout a guide.

We all need to become more culturally aware, regardless of our native cultures, mainstream or not, so that we can see the perspectives of others, so that no one will have to take that uncomfortable stance and step in. Yet, it is important for librarians, especially from nonmainstream populations to feel they have a voice and can speak up when they feel that diversity is not visible because that is how we can effect positive change.

Summary

Training staff to become culturally competent takes energy, patience, and buy-in. Effective training includes developing rapport, trust, and confidentiality with the participants. In addition to training, the bigger diversity plan should also have action steps in place to see that continued efforts are being made to assist the library as a whole in being a culturally competent library. Those characteristics include committing to these points:

1. an awareness and acceptance of cultural differences
2. an attention to the dynamic cultural differences
3. recruitment and retention of minority library staff
4. continuous adaptation of service models for the needs of people from diverse cultures
5. constant evaluation of library staff and policies concerning cultures

CHAPTER EIGHT

Library School Curriculum Reform and Diversity

One of the major findings in this study is that librarians gain their master's degree in library and information studies with very little training or coursework in multicultural librarianship. As a result, they usually enter their positions with a limited cultural lens and provide services from a monocultural reference point. Librarians who accept positions to coordinate diversity efforts not only need to educate themselves to become more culturally competent, but also need to develop approaches to motivate others to learn to be more culturally aware. This chapter provides some of the curriculum issues in library schools and suggestions for reforming it to provide some foundational cultural knowledge for future librarians by interweaving diversity awareness and elements in each class.

Recruitment of Students of Color to Library Schools

There has been much written about issues and attempts to diversify library staff and to attract more students of color to library schools. Although the focus of this book is not to detail those efforts, a summary of some of the issues that lead minorities not to consider attending library school is relevant to further point to the need to train all librarians to work with diverse cultures.

Much of the literature focuses on the difficulty library schools encounter when trying to recruit academically strong and ethnically diverse students. Library school programs are competing with graduate programs in other disciplines such as business administration, engineering, computer science, medicine, and law. Adkins and Espinal (2004) also attribute a lack of interest in library positions to low salaries, lack of minority professors, and lack of minority library science programs.

According to the Association for Library and Information Science Education (ALISE) statistical reports (2007), the student population enrolled in the master's program at library and information science (LIS) schools and programs has not been as ethnically diverse as the U.S. population. Among the students enrolled in American Library Association (ALA)–accredited LIS schools, only 11.85% are ethnic minorities including the four main groups: African Americans, American Indians, Asian Americans, and Hispanic Americans. This proportion is significantly lower than the proportion of minorities enrolled in graduate programs (26.4%) overall and those in the U.S. population (31.3%) (U.S. Bureau of Census, 2000). It will be interesting to see if this trend has shifted when the next census reports these data.

LIS schools have been active in efforts to provide incentives for minority students to enroll in their programs. ALA created the Spectrum Initiative in 1997 to promote diversity in the library community and recruit minority librarians by providing scholarships, mentoring, and training programs. Various ALA groups also offer scholarships, such as one from the Black Caucus of the American Library Association. Another means of support is available through programs of the Institute of Museum and Library Services (IMLS). This program assists LIS students of color through scholarship and recruitment programs such as Knowledge River and PRAXIS (Practice, Reflection, Advocacy, Excellence, Inquiry, Solutions) (Josey, 1993).

These efforts offer opportunities for library schools to increase their representation of students of color and to provide needed perspectives to the programs. However, the progress is slow, with a considerable gap between the enrolled students and the U.S. population. Even with increased representation of people of color in the profession, librarians of color will still make up only a small percentage of librarians working with students of color. Library schools need to think of efforts to develop and implement effective programs to train all librarians to be effective communicators, instructors, and advocates to and for students of color. All graduates need to be prepared to work in larger multicultural environments. This next section will provide some results from the survey and interviews that detail some of the issues perceived by the librarians in the study and their views on how library schools should enhance their curriculum.

Curriculum Issues: What Are We Teaching?

It is important for all students enrolled in LIS programs to be exposed to issues of multiculturalism and diversity. Students with an interest in this area will usually self-select and enroll in courses that have a broader cultural perspective. Students who do not necessarily hold such an interest will usually apply their precious credit hours to taking other courses. However, in many instances, upon graduation the latter students may find themselves ill prepared for encounters with library patrons who are very different from themselves. These graduates may possess little knowledge of how best to respond to and to bridge those differences. There are certain approaches that may be used to help maximize such outcomes, such as an entire course devoted to diversity issues in LIS education. Other possibilities include organizing units in a given course (e.g., reference, cataloging, collection development) around multicultural or diversity issues and inviting guest speakers to discuss topics such as collection development, gay and lesbian literature, or concerns of library service and programming for older adults. Peterson (1995) suggests these and other strategies for infusing the LIS curriculum in an effort to reach the largest number of students. She also makes the important point that multiple efforts must be made concurrently if multicultural education in the LIS curriculum is to touch every student at some level during his or her program of study.

This approach may be necessary because few schools of library and information science offer full courses on diversity issues and few LIS faculty maintain a teaching or research focus in these areas. Of the 54 U.S. library schools, only 30 list faculty with a research or teaching specialty of service to multicultural populations (Association for Library and Information Science Education, 2007). Of that number, only 22 schools have faculty who may teach courses related to multicultural populations, and four of those individuals are adjunct faculty. Also of note is that only 62 of over 2,000 full- and part-time faculty listed a teaching or research specialty of serving multicultural populations. About half of those were from San José State University. These small numbers suggest that library schools should be attempting a more organized and deliberate effort in multicultural education.

Interviewees shared some reflections concerning their training in multicultural education while working on their masters in library and information science:

An African American librarian in the study said

> I went to graduate school at [a Midwestern university] and
> I had a fellowship for an institute. The Institute trained

minority students to become librarians and what they were calling community college resource learning centers at the time. So it was probably about 20 of us, maybe more, pretty evenly divided among African-Americans and Latinos and that was the most minority students I've ever seen at graduate school and we took regular library science classes and then we had classes in the school of education and special seminars about working in community colleges with diverse populations and for the work that we would do in the community college. I don't think that the library schools are doing that anymore. I think they do just multicultural bibliography types of things. Our training was specifically geared. That was one of the things that was drilled into us in library school in the Institute classes and the classes in the school of education - that we would be working with nontraditional diverse populations and that we needed to look for new ways of meeting these people's needs.

A Native American librarian mentioned:

I'm really happy overall with my library education, but it was very theoretical. There was no middle ground in terms of that. I'm trying to think of the courses I took and they really didn't focus on services to different populations. I went into library school with a strong social justice background of what I wanted to do. It happened that I was living in [name of state] at the time. So what I did was an independent study with the professor working at a tribal college library in [name of state]. That's when I really realized that this is something that I was interested in.

An Anglo American librarian commented, "I think that classes should include skills in cross-cultural communication. That's a big one. I didn't get any of that actually. I am picking up by watching and observing."

Courses with Multicultural Components
The respondents to the librarian survey stated that there should be more emphasis on multicultural awareness and training in library schools.

Their choices of ways to do this are documented in Figures 8.1 and 8.2.

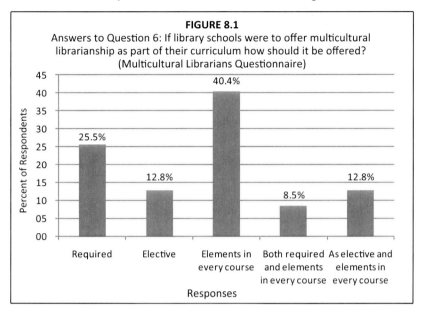

FIGURE 8.1
Answers to Question 6: If library schools were to offer multicultural librarianship as part of their curriculum how should it be offered? (Multicultural Librarians Questionnaire)

Although a quarter of the respondents felt that a specific course should be required, more (40.4%) indicated that a more comprehensive approach would be to add elements in every course. Some follow-up responses in the interviews confirmed this.

An African American female said, "I think there needs to be some diversity component in every course and faculty need to communicate to the students it's becoming a more diverse area. They need to know how to locate resources across all disciplines and understand populations even in cataloging. Talk about how Library of Congress subject headings might not work as well. All the way through the curriculum." Another said, "I agree that this should be more of a priority in Library school. However, I feel library school, in general, is very limited toward meeting the sorts of goals that multicultural outreach demands."

A Hispanic American librarian mentioned, "I'm working with the librarian's group devoted to increasing diversity in academic libraries. Once more libraries and library school personnel understand the issues, they'll influence their libraries and MLIS programs to find a way to recruit more diverse librarians and library students." Another said, "Library schools need to offer or include services to diverse communities into all courses. We are no longer 'a nation of one size fits all' when it comes to library services."

Outreach and Community Service

Some library programs offer opportunities to get out into the communities and work with disadvantaged populations to help bring them library services. A librarian working on a reservation felt that more librarians and library school students need to understand that part of our obligation is to explore those areas where we can help extend library services, or at least to understand that they exist and that not everyone has the same access. A Native American remarked:

> Librarians—God bless them. We really believe in what we do, but I think we spend a lot of the time preaching to the choir, so I wish there were some element in a course somewhere that said that everybody doesn't have libraries. Everybody doesn't have these options and we think that just because there are libraries all over they are being used and utilized and appreciated and that they are meeting the needs of people. But they're not all the time. And that's something that I discovered through my own work on the reservation, not in school. A little bit of that theoretical, it might pique people's interest to say, 'Hey I believe in libraries and getting involved in different ways.'

A Hispanic American shared:

> In Library school one of our first classes was Knowledge River working with Latinos and Native Americans. That wasn't so much dealing with cultural aspects but challenges that these groups are facing. I think it's very difficult for people to imagine not having any water, or any electricity. The perception that everyone has access to the Internet somewhere. If someone tells you that on a certain reservation that there's no electricity, you might say 'Wow. What are you talking about? This is 2008. How can there not be electricity or running water?' If you don't get told those types of things you don't really know. I was lucky that as part of Knowledge River we had different classes that might be a little different from the

traditional library school classes where you would have once a semester a different class focusing on multicultural issues. It may not be cultural as with social norms, but more focusing on challenges, issues and history. With the exposure, you have to learn that on your own.

Another librarian said:

I took an Outreach class at Rutgers, which opened up the field to me. I think in today's world all new librarians should have a similar class under their belts. Also cultural differences and nuances, instead of Human Information Behavior classes focusing on doctors, lawyers and such, and an information-searching behavior class related to different ethnic groups, etc., would be more helpful.

Collection Development

Collection development is one area that typically introduces the need to consider various ethnic groups and collections during the selection process. There are also some courses in library schools that are entirely devoted to a particular ethnic group. Many of these are in schools in the southwest or in areas with large concentrations of non-mainstream ethnic communities. Not everyone goes to library school thinking they will be involved in collection development, so they may not take those courses. Even fewer take the dedicated course for a particular population unless their goal is to work with that population. Following are several comments made by librarians in the study regarding collection development education.

- "I believe that having an extensive background in the foundations of collection development is extremely helpful for a person who endeavors to be a so-termed multicultural librarian!"
- "Librarianship is traditionally a profession concerned with selecting, collecting, and making accessible a balance of information resources representing all knowledge relative to the mission without censorship. Traditionally, we have always provided professional information service to all users within the group for which a library is established. Diversity and cultural information exists in the books and resources of nearly every library even without special effort to collect them specifically.

Today, there are growing, rather than diminishing needs for a more directed collecting and service provision related to racial, cultural, religious, and social diversity."

- "I wish collection development really had been covered. Building a collection is really different than evaluating a collection and seeing what's there and trying to find holes. Maybe that's too practical of a subject to be covered, but that's one of the many challenges to cover. It's not a skill that you immediately know how to do and how to evaluate. They had a collection development course, but it was more like you develop a collection. You pick a subject from scratch and develop one. But there wasn't a lot of talk about how you evaluate a collection in your library. And how you look at the collection and try to find holes or what sort of things you buy (like DVDs). It's one thing to build a collection from scratch, but not looking at the existing collection."

- "When you're selecting you're selecting for everybody and you need to be looking for the materials from other cultures and stuff. But the reality is that you get all, well, I don't want to call it bogged down, but you have to select for so many other things that the diversity stuff gets the short shrift. The way we're set up we have the approval process and you go down and look at the approval books. But a lot of times unless somebody set up the profile to include that kind of stuff and the publishers, those books never come into the approval process. So somebody had to be out there looking for them."

- "We need to have more of those classes that deal with specific resources and like reference resources in diverse areas and to help them to know how to evaluate the resources they have. That whole area of focus in reference and learning environments really needs to be expanded in library school."

When assessing the extent to which aspects or components of multicultural librarianship or education are actually integrated into the curriculum, some of the librarians surveyed could remember instances where there was some effort to discuss these issues in the classes, but most of them could not recall any. However, respondents of the library school survey indicated that this is something that is done. As noted in figure 8.2, at least 44% of the respondents from the library school survey indicated that faculty make a conscious effort to include diversity components in a course.

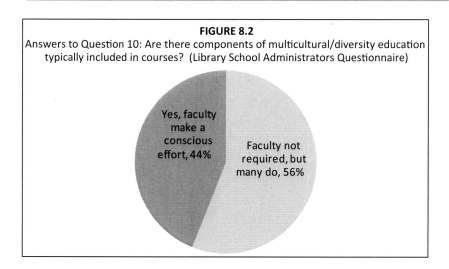

FIGURE 8.2
Answers to Question 10: Are there components of multicultural/diversity education typically included in courses? (Library School Administrators Questionnaire)

Unfortunately, since this was an anonymous survey, it was not possible to compare these responses to the actual library schools. That comparison might indicate if this was a practice more common to schools in ethnically diverse areas. Another question that could have been asked is whether or not faculty were required to include diversity components. The next section will provide some of the suggestions for modifying courses.

Modifying Courses: Recommendations from the Literature

In a study done with human resource (HR) managers to determine their graduate preparation for diversity (Day and Glick, 2000), HR managers indicated that they wanted more emphasis on communication and listening skills, team building, and international diversity issues. In their courses, however, more emphasis was placed on how to manage diversity within specific demographic groups. This study concluded that course content should reflect the organizational demands and include components that will be needed on the job. Similarly, library schools should also take into consideration what the organizational demands for diversity are and modify their curriculum accordingly. In addition to providing a historical background and collection development strategies for diverse groups, they should be thinking about how to prepare librarians to effectively interact with others, no matter where they might be in the library organization. To that end, there have been several suggestions for redesigning curriculum in library schools, which will be discussed in the following sections.

Researcher Recommendations

Researchers and faculty have long provided suggestions for modifying the LIS curriculum in order to better prepare future librarians (Kim and Sei-Ching, 2008; Peterson, 2005; Wheeler, 2005; Lillard and Wales, 2003; Roy, 2001; Chu, 2002; Gollop, 1999; Talbot and Kocarek, 1997; Nance-Mitchell, 1996; Talbot, 1996; Arzu, 1995; East and Lam, 1995; Freiband, 1992). They suggest that students need more training to better prepare them to effectively interact and communicate with diverse students, to plan programs that meet their needs, and to support their growth and development.

Raju (2003) surveyed past students, employers, and educators in the LIS field in South Africa to gather data on their views of the core courses offered for their LIS degree. Of particular interest here are suggestions made for other skills and knowledge that should be included in LIS programs. They include cultural diversity, customer care, communication skills, interpersonal skills, library advocacy, community and development work, and project management. All of these skills are needed by not only librarians coordinating multicultural programming, but by any librarian who comes into contact with other individuals.

ALA Recommendations

ALA indicated the need to infuse cultural competency and diversity elements into the curriculum as well. In 2007, the ALA Committee on Diversity (American Library Association, 2007, p. 31) recommended that section 60.0 of the ALA Policy on Diversity be revised to include goals for inclusive and culturally competent library and information services (60.4). The goals make concrete what libraries have been striving to accomplish for quite some time:

> 60.4 Goals for Inclusive and Culturally Competent Library and Information Services
>
> Cultural competency is defined as the acceptance and respect for diversity, continuing self-assessment regarding culture, and the ongoing development of knowledge, resources, and service models that work towards effectively meeting the needs of diverse populations. Cultural competence is critical to the equitable provision of library and information services; therefore, the

American Library Association urges library personnel to commit themselves to the following guidelines.

1. To ensure equitable services to every community member or group, training and ongoing education that promote awareness of and sensitivity to diversity must be stressed for all library personnel.
2. Care must be taken to acquire and provide materials that meet the educational, informational, and recreational needs of diverse communities.
3. Efforts to identify and eliminate cultural, economic, literacy-related, linguistic, physical, technological, or perceptional barriers that limit access to library and information resources must be prioritized and ongoing.
4. The creation of library services and delivery operations, which will ensure rapid access to information in a manner reflective of the communities they serve.
5. A diverse workforce is essential to the provision of competent library services. A concerted effort must be undertaken to recruit and retain diverse personnel at every level of the library workforce. Opportunities for career advancement must also be available to these individuals.
6. To ensure the development and enhancement of library services to diverse populations, library personnel from diverse and underrepresented backgrounds must be encouraged to take active roles in the American Library Association and other professional library organizations.

Now that these goals constitute ALA policy, what kind of support exists for working towards them? Lack of training continues to impede progress. Libraries have attempted to address at least goals 1 through 5 for some time and with varying degrees of success. Accomplishing these goals should be of utmost priority since they would help reestablish individuals to coordinate diversity initiatives at libraries. However, to make rapid headway, librarians need to come into the profession with at least foundational knowledge on becoming culturally competent.

Along with the aforementioned revision, there was also a revision to section 60.5 (Library Education to Meet the Needs of a Diverse Society).

The last part of the statement specifically addresses the need for curriculum in LIS programs to include diversity components. The goal states: "The American Library Association, through the Committee on Accreditation, will encourage graduate library and information science programs seeking accreditation or re-accreditation 'to ensure that their student bodies, faculties, and curricula [author's emphasis] reflect the diverse histories and information needs of all people in the United States.... '" (p. XX). Educating future librarians to recognize the contributions and information needs of diverse populations is critical and a good first step for curriculum-planning reform. What is lacking, though, is the commitment to assist future librarians in becoming culturally competent (as was defined by ALA in 60.4 above). In doing so, library school curriculum should include examples and training of cross-cultural communication, cultural sensitivity, differing service models, and working with diverse populations.

An example of an effort to train library school students to become culturally competent is the Librarians for Tomorrow Project (Somerville and Yusko, 2008), a joint effort of San José State University, San José Public Library, and the San José State University School of Library and Information Science. This grant-funded project is aimed at recruiting and training librarians from underserved communities to learn how to best serve cultural communities. The project provides funding for coursework, attendance at conferences, and coaching to help the librarians to become more culturally competent and eventual leaders of diversity efforts. The curriculum at the library school has been specifically modified for these individuals to allow them to focus on courses that will best assist them in learning how to provide the optimum service to underserved communities. They also participate in two internship courses that place them in a library with a high percentage of users from underserved populations. If this project proves successful, it could be a model for other library schools, not just for students from underserved populations, but for students in general.

Adding Multicultural Components

Even if there isn't a set diversity program or curriculum in place at library schools, there are many options for increasing the multicultural or diversity awareness of students in a course with relatively little effort. One is to invite guest speakers (either virtually or in person) from diverse cultures to share their experiences using libraries. Elturk (2003) emphasizes the value of consulting individuals from the various cultural groups in order to gain authenticity and to avoid "cultural appropriation," which is the adoption of some specific elements of one culture by a different cultural group. It is important to consult with individuals from the native culture to make sure that there are no misrepresentations or divergent meanings when referring to cultural nuances. Consulting with individuals from specific cultural groups and inviting them in to speak can provide authenticity. They may be able to include relevant strategies for ways to communicate and interact that would help in making the librarian and library seem more approachable. They could also share their perception of the strengths and weaknesses of library collections and services and suggestions for improvements. These dialogues allow students to hear what it is like from someone actively working with diversity issues or someone from a background other than the mainstream. Oftentimes the talks result in subsequent opportunities to reflect upon scenarios and ways to rethink the provision of services. Another easy way to incorporate diversity in courses is to include readings from the viewpoint of ethnic minorities and authors. Rather than always choosing readings from the mainstream population, one could seek out some of the leaders in the field who are outside of the mainstream population. There are also many multimedia tools available, such as YouTube, that can be used to provide some training sessions for working with diverse populations in almost any area.

This "integration approach" to providing diversity education would be most effective if done in a coordinated effort. If not, students may learn about only the topics that are of interest to the particular faculty member teaching the course or that could easily or naturally be introduced into the course. It does not assure that every student will receive the necessary knowledge needed to be culturally competent. By developing coordination between courses related to diversity education, students may begin to reflect more deeply on the necessity to reframe their thinking and procedures.

Diversity Integration Plan

Flowers (2003) recommends that graduate programs create a "diversity integration plan." This plan would look at the various courses offered and suggest components for diversity knowledge to be incorporated into that course. Flowers provides some examples for integration, such as introducing theories of racial identity and identity development in theory courses. For every course, a diversity component could be added, whether for instructional practices, reference interactions, research design, technology development, cataloging, administration, or policy studies. Specifics would need to be developed for how the courses would provide education that allows students to raise their level of self-awareness, improve authentic cross-cultural knowledge, improve cross-cultural communication, modify and apply cultural considerations into their practice, and learn how to assess the library and campus climate and develop plans to improve areas. Along with a diversity integration plan, some exit interview or assessment might be offered to assess whether the students have developed adequate cultural competencies.

Abdullahi (2007) also argues that library schools should plan for systematic inclusion of intercultural issues within the curriculum. He discusses four characteristics that the curriculum should help students to develop: sociocultural consciousness, an affirming attitude towards students from diverse backgrounds, commitment and skills to act as agents of change, and culturally responsive teaching practices. This framework would be far reaching and would no doubt take much planning and time to actualize, including the reeducation of library school faculty to help them develop these skills. Even if this isn't totally implemented, at a minimum the values and skills he addresses should be seriously considered by library schools.

Summary

Courses in library schools attempt to connect the relevance of the content material to various areas of librarianship. In doing so, each course should be interspersing multicultural education components as they relate to the content. According to U.S. Census projections (2008), whites will be a minority in this country by 2050. This is one compelling reason to include multicultural education in all courses, for each librarian will no doubt be working with other cultures, no matter which library or position they are in. They may not intentionally seek a position with a focus on multicultural librarianship, but they will at minimum be working with others who may have different views, perspectives, experiences, communication styles, interaction styles, and expectations. Many librarians, even those outside of public services, serve as liaisons to other groups. Any librarian who comes in contact with another individual, either face to face or virtually, can benefit from learning about other cultures, norms, expectations, and communication styles. By consciously extending the content in each course to reflect on what some of the issues or strategies might be for working with different populations, students may begin to think more broadly about their actions and reactions.

CHAPTER NINE

Next Steps: How to Strengthen Diversity Efforts

To strengthen library services to diverse populations, library schools should enhance their curriculum to include cultural diversity components so that future librarians begin their careers with some foundational knowledge of and sensitivity and awareness towards other cultures. Library administrators should also take a more direct and active role in supporting librarians working towards becoming more culturally competent. This chapter will first provide examples of motivational factors for these librarians and follow with ideas for library administrators to augment their diversity efforts.

What Motivates Us

Previous chapters in this book provided some of the experiences, perspectives, and suggestions of librarians working to coordinate diversity efforts in their libraries. Although the overall impression may appear to be that individuals in these roles are fighting an uphill battle, these librarians also expressed strong motivations to continue in their efforts. Even though these librarians encountered challenges in their efforts to promote cultural diversity and to establish relationships with their constituencies, they also found rewarding aspects of their jobs. The next section will provide ways in which they were motivated. Most commented on the benefits of having a flexible (autonomous) job and the intrinsic rewards and gratification of their work.

Autonomy

Autonomy on the job was one of the most positive aspects of the job for most of the librarians in this study, with 93.8% indicating they were very satisfied or mostly satisfied, as long as there was also support (see figure 4.3). A common factor for most of these librarians is that they are allowed to design the job as needed in order to accomplish their duties and goals. One librarian was very positive about her experience because she was given free rein to set the program up as needed. Her supervisor told her, "We want the library and its university to continue to have fun. Go do whatever you need to do." She has had tremendous support and felt like she has never been "twisting in the wind out there." That was a real relief to her. Other librarians view their wide range of responsibilities as an unexpected benefit of their positions, rather than as unexpected (and often unwelcome) added duties. Figure 4.3 provides the level of satisfaction these librarians had with autonomy on the job.

Intrinsic Rewards

As noted above, most librarians were satisfied with the autonomy they felt they had in their job, which can contribute to feeling intrinsically rewarded. Intrinsic work values are to factors such as having a job that permits one to develop one's own methods of doing work, is intellectually stimulating, provides change and variety in duties, and provides a feeling of accomplishment. Factors such as a job that permits advancement to high administrative responsibility, opportunity for higher income, and comfortable working conditions represent extrinsic work values. Librarians in this study frequently mentioned satisfaction in areas that would indicate that they are rewarded intrinsically for their efforts, such as their autonomy on the job and also a sense of accomplishment in doing what they felt was important.

Some of the sense of accomplishment was in the form of personal interactions with others. Many reflections by interviewees focused on the personal satisfaction they feel by helping others and with the connections and friendships created by reaching out to others. They shared the satisfaction of developing a long-term mentoring type of relationship, including the struggles and achievements of students as they progressed through college. These librarians were outgoing, people-centered, and interested in personal achievements, both by themselves and others. One of the joys they expressed was seeing how helping others can positively affect their studies, outlook, goals, and success.

Another common area of accomplishment expressed was the progress of the multicultural work of other library staff as they took on new roles, shared in creating new services, or extended existing services to a more diverse user group. For some, it was the active participation of others that provided the recognition and intrinsic rewards they sought for their own

efforts. Cardelle-Elawar and Nevin (2003) discuss what motivates teachers in their work, and what is said applies to librarians who connect with
others in that they also engage in their work for personal growth, fulfill-
ment, self-determination, and a desire to achieve. They also suggest that a
major characteristic of achievement-oriented people is that they seem to be
more concerned with personal achievement than with rewards. Although
monetary compensation is a critical factor in attracting and retaining
exemplary employees, as Hersey, Blanchard, and Johnson (2001) point
out , as individuals become more concerned with esteem, recognition,
and eventually self-actualization, money becomes a less motivating tool
(p. 42). Eventually intrinsic satisfaction plays the greater role in motivation. Daugherty et al. (2003) suggest that individuals who perceive that
rewards are contingent on their own behavior as opposed to controlled
by outside forces are in the long run the most effective teachers (p. 152).
Pressley and Roehrig (2004) also noted the importance for satisfaction for
those that place more focus on a cognitive individual and intrinsic reward.

Following are some of the reflections of the librarians who were
interviewed regarding the benefits and positive aspects of what they do.
One person's motivation was seeing the library become a more welcoming environment: "I think for us, we wanted to make sure we were being
inclusive. We want the diverse community to walk into the library and
see this as a library where I feel welcomed, and that's your primary goal.
It's part of your public service to the patron. I looked at it as an open
place." Another reflected that she felt "a sense of purpose." Other comments included these:

- "I love my work and I'm happy to have this position. This
  job really appealed to me because I really wanted to work in
  something like this and I didn't want to be ensconced in an
  office."
- "I guess I feel recognized for what I'm doing and my reward is
  actually making a difference, which I can see. And that's at the
  heart of why I do this. I know there's a lot of talk about diversity
  here, and most of it is not lip service at all. So I know that the
  people I work with, and I mean the university, think that what
  I'm doing is valuable, and that's enough for me."
- "The reward is that people do value that, the population that
  you work with. It's gratifying to hear them say sincerely, 'Thank
  you.' That is rewarding. You go to adult orientation, and they do

their survey about what areas of the University they feel really good about and the libraries is always one of the best. That helps. And of course when you're doing your orientation, you're not doing anything anybody else couldn't have done, but you are just welcoming them to the University and what's there for them. But it's just to know that there is support, and there's somebody there. It is rewarding to know that they appreciate that."

Many of these librarians feel a personal satisfaction that results from self-actualization. Their intrinsic motivation leads to autonomy and accountability to themselves and to others. Some are also gratified to have a leadership role, which fosters their personal satisfaction and professional accountability. In positions where the leader is a change agent, they have the opportunity to inspire and motivate staff to achieve high, self-imposed standards as well.

Suggestions for Library Administrators
Advocating for Diversity Efforts

Not all libraries are able to hire designated individuals to lead diversity efforts. For those that are, administrators cannot afford to step away and leave them to figure out the job on their own. Regardless of whether or not a library has a designated individual, if the library wants to promote diversity education, administrators will need to be strong advocates. As already stated, there must be a commitment to multicultural inclusiveness, and the tone must be established by the upper administration. This includes investing resources (time and money) to support diversity training and other efforts. Administrators need to make sure that all staff are held accountable for working towards creating as inclusive an environment as possible, beginning with diversity training. When asked, "What would you like the library directors to know?" one interviewee said "I think that it is that the position has to be considered a vital part of the library, to be accepted and deemed important. The structure and the foundation have to be there."

Williams (1999) advises library leaders to approach the library's diversity agenda with patience, optimism, creativity, persistence, a bias for input and assessment, an aversion to perfection, a willingness to learn from failure, a responsiveness in the face of discomfort and disagreement, a willingness to present and pursue multiple options and rationales to advance diversity, a willingness to pursue multiple starting points for action, and a willingness to rethink organizational structures in order to advance the library's diversity program.

Librarians in this study also commented that they wish administrators would not automatically look to put the minority librarians on every library committee, work group, or initiative that was related to diversity. Although the librarians recognize the value of these contributions, they are very time-consuming, take away from the official job duties, and may yield very little to the tenure process, or even have a negative impact. Although representation is important, librarians of color can be used in consultancy roles to assist others in taking on advocacy roles on behalf of diverse cultures.

Even if a library is fortunate to have a librarian to lead diversity efforts and if this librarian is from a minority culture, administrators cannot expect this person to be the sole individual representing diversity or diverse cultures. Recruitment and retention of librarians of color should still be a priority of library administration. Although the goal should be to have every librarian become culturally competent, it is still important to have a staff that reflects the diversity of the community being served.

Recruitment for Jobs

One of the areas of recruitment in which administrators can be more actively engaged is the recruitment of librarians of color to their library. With so few librarians of color available, it might take special efforts to entice them to even take a second look at a library that might be geographically or culturally very different from where they were raised. There are various techniques for recruiting that can be used. In addition to using available communication tools such as electronic discussion lists, professional networks, personal contacts, professional publications and promoting the library and community whenever possible, there are other methods. These include making qualifications flexible and open; making the search and recruitment processes more efficient; utilizing signing bonuses, higher salaries, and creative compensation packages; holding open houses; traveling to job fairs and library schools to recruit; mentoring student workers; and emphasizing the importance of librarian and staff roles in the recruiting process (Kaufman, 2002). The next section discusses another area of recruitment that is necessary in order to motivate people of color to consider entering the profession.

Recruitment to the Profession

As Alire (1997) points out, "One way to serve minority communities better is to hire minority staff who not only can relate and understand diverse cultures, but who can also serve as role models to attract nonusers" (p. 39). Having a culturally diverse staff can significantly increase the comfort level of library patrons with different ethnic, racial, and religious backgrounds. They are more prone to seek assistance from library staff they can relate to and who they feel will empathize with their information needs and experiences (Gandhi, 2000; Adkins and Espinal 2004). One librarian in the study remarked, "Approaching someone who shares their cultural background—it's like a magnetic connection, and something that goes deeper than words. It can also be as superficial as feeling safer approaching someone who looks like you."

Librarians can also look to their support staff, encourage them to pursue their degrees, and help them throughout the process.

Recruitment to Library School

There are various recruitment efforts underway for library schools, which is important if libraries hope to see a growth in the number of librarians of color in the profession. Library administrators have an opportunity to partner with some of these programs and even host events at their institution to help promote the library profession to undergraduates. Over the last few decades, LIS schools and programs have worked diligently to recruit people of color into the information profession, and other related organizations also have been active in supporting recruitment programs. The Spectrum Initiative Scholarship program, for example, created by ALA in 1997, promotes diversity in the library community and helps to recruit minority librarians by providing scholarships, mentoring, and training programs. Several LIS schools support the Spectrum Initiative scholarship program by agreeing to make additional financial commitments to the effort by either matching grants or supplementing them. The Institute of Museum and Library Services (IMLS) since 1996 has also helped LIS schools increase the number of students of color through scholarships, recruitment programs such as Knowledge River and PRAXIS (Practice, Reflection, Advocacy, Excellence, Inquiry, Solutions), and other initiatives.

Other programs that assist with library school tuition are the Prism Fellowship program and the Mellon Foundation. The Prism Fellowship program gives future professionals from underrepresented groups work experience and library school tuition. The Mellon Foundation provides grants for the Mellon Librarian Recruitment Program for undergraduate students at Atlanta University, Mount Holyoke, Oberlin, Occidental, Swarthmore, and Wellesley. They usually include internships, library science career awareness, and scholarships.

There are other ways that college and university libraries can be actively involved in developing and promoting efforts to recruit future librarians. Various college and university libraries develop undergraduate internships to encourage low-income and ethnic minority students to enter the library profession. Some of these include the California State University, Bakersfield; the Diversity Internship in Libraries Program, sponsored by the University of Massachusetts-Boston, Simmons College Libraries; and the Simmons Graduate School of Library and Information Science, (which exposes high-school students to the profession through internships). The University of Arizona's School of Information Resources and Library Science actively recruits minority students into its Knowledge River program and provides them with an extensive support network, financial assistance, and culturally sensitive educational opportunities. The University of Arizona has also had success with its Peer Information Counseling program. This program recruits undergraduate minority and international students and provides them with technology training. The students are also trained to do a number of tasks, including instruction, presentations, and reference. It provides them a chance to learn about the profession and hopefully motivates them to go onto library school.

Residency and Fellowship Programs

University librarians can be more directly involved with recruitment efforts through the establishment of residency programs. Several university libraries that provide minority residency programs are at Cornell University; Iowa State University; Miami University in Oxford, Ohio, Ohio State University; the University of Michigan; and Yale University. Indiana University's School of Library and Information Science has a database of minority residencies. Some of the schools involved are Auburn University, Cornell University, North Carolina State University, the University of Delaware, the University of Tennessee, the University of Arizona, and the University of Pittsburgh. All of the programs are paid and range from one to two years. The salaries are usually competitive, and some offer an incentive like reimbursement of relocation costs. Most programs provide a "home" department where the librarian is fully integrated as a member of the professional staff. In addition to a salary and tuition break, many institutions also provide a professional development stipend to attend conferences and training.

Libraries that are close to library schools should collaborate with library schools to provide residency programs. These have the benefit of attracting individuals who can earn their library degrees at the same time as doing the residency. The residency program was designed to give new librarians a chance to experience different areas of librarianship, not just the multicultural part of it. Several of the librarians interviewed for this study had been residents, which gave them grounding in various aspects of librarianship. Most of them stayed at the institutions where they held their residency, although that is generally not a requirement. Some institutions provide staff of color the opportunity to earn their library degrees while still employed at the library. In most cases they created a residency program that allowed the staff member the experiences of working in roles more in line with those of a professional librarian.

Residency and fellowship programs provide invaluable career development opportunities to new library professionals, as well as ways for libraries to achieve their objectives (Brewer, 2001).

Retention Efforts

It is interesting to note that, while initiatives to recruit minority librarians are widely reported in the literature, very little emphasis is placed on the retention of these librarians. Job satisfaction and intrinsic satisfactions are areas that administrators can monitor in hopes of providing a work environment and duties that will motivate librarians to stay. Lester and Kickul (2001) found an organization's ability to fulfill an employee's expectation towards intrinsic and extrinsic rewards to be significantly related to factors such as job satisfaction and intention to leave. They found the inability of an organization to meet an employee's expected intrinsic and extrinsic rewards to be negatively associated with job satisfaction and positively associated with intention to leave.

The following observation made by Martin (1994) about minority students on academic campuses also rings true for minority librarians: "Students [librarians] of color experience frustration when they are recruited by institutions on the strengths of their previous achievements and cultural affiliations but then are expected to become like Euro-American students [librarians] with whom they have little in common" (p. 2). Both recruitment and retention of minority librarians can be successful only if there is a realization that people are different from each other and that minority librarians, despite being different in their looks, mannerisms, and ways of doing things, nevertheless do have certain strengths and are capable of making significant contributions to the profession. Libraries will benefit enormously by learning from the different perspectives, communication patterns, and skills that minority librarians bring to the profession.

The retention of minority librarians can also be greatly enhanced with the development of effective mentoring programs that will guide them through the rough spots and help them acquire a broad range of experiences. Such programs will increase the skills and confidence of minority librarians. However, increased skills and expertise are valuable only if there are avenues for minority librarians to progress in their career paths and move into management positions. According to Thomas (1990), "Women and minorities no longer need a boarding pass, they need an upgrade. The problem is not getting them at the entry level; the problem is making better use of their potential at every level, especially in middle management and leadership positions" (p. 107). He adds, "Getting hired is not the problem [for minorities].... It's later on that many of them plateau and lose their drive and quit or get fired. It's later on that their manager's inability to manage diversity hobbles them." (p. 107). Although this was written almost 20 years ago, librarians of color in this study echoed this same barrier to moving up the ladder. If librarians are hoping to climb the career ladders to leadership and management levels and they are overlooked, they may lose their motivation and desire to excel. That then may result in their leaving the institution or failing to get tenure. Therefore, it is vital that for diversity initiatives in libraries to be successful, the focus should not only be on hiring minority librarians, but also on grooming them for and promoting them to leadership positions within library organizations (Gandhi, 2000).

Another effort that library administrators can pursue that can contribute to retention is to establish mentors for new librarians, especially for librarians who are in positions that are very autonomous and without a lot of traditional structure.

Mentoring

Mentoring, a "dynamic reciprocal relationship in a work environment between an advanced career incumbent and a beginner aimed at promoting the career development of both" (Healy, 1997, p. 10), can be an effective method for assisting librarians to learn of the culture of a library and to feel they are part of a network. Kaufman (2002, p. 4) sums up some important aspects of mentoring: "Mentoring takes time, lots of time, and it takes the courage to open doors for 'mentees' and encourages them to walk through them, on paths that are different than we have taken, to heights and parts unknown. In today's and tomorrow's worlds mentoring can make the difference between success and failure to lead; it can make the difference between developing people to succeed us successfully or letting the chips fall where they may."

The Need for Designated Librarians to Coordinate Diversity Efforts

One of the questions asked of the participants in this study was whether or not they thought there needed to be a designated librarian to coordinate diversity efforts. Given that there are relatively few of these librarians, as well as the challenges libraries have encountered in their attempts to hire them, one wonders if these tasks can be successfully divided among other librarians. Librarians felt that there needed to be an individual who could look at the big picture as well as where there are gaps that need to be filled in. If the training, grant writing, liaison work, collection development, instruction, outreach, programming, mentoring, and hand holding that goes with this job were split among various librarians, they feared that the focus towards individuals from underrepresented cultures would be much less. Diversity committees, assuming there is one at the library, then becomes responsible for all of the training and programming. Yet these librarians do this work in addition to all of their regular work and are not able to place as much priority on the efforts. Additionally, students of color may be more inclined to approach someone if they have been in touch with them individually at various venues and feel as though they are part of the community. They may be less inclined to contact a member of a diversity committee. Assessment of efforts is also something that a diversity librarian can attend to in a programmatic way.

Anderson (1993) identified six areas of diversity that promote a sense of community and should be maintained by ongoing assessment. The six areas are (1) frequency and focus of student–faculty non-classroom interaction, (2) nature of peer group interaction and extracurricular activities, (3) quality of teaching, (4) extent to which institutional structures facilitate student academic and social involvement, (5) curricular experiences and effective general education, and (6) coursework patterns. It really takes a designated individual, such as a diversity librarian, to oversee that these areas are being addressed.

Summary

Improving the institutional climate and learning experiences of the library's constituencies is an important goal for libraries. Being aware of and knowledgeable about other cultures can help individuals from those cultures view the library as a welcoming place and be more inclined to use those services. However, it takes the effort of every individual in the library to be willing to learn how to make interactions more culturally responsive. While recruitment of librarians of color is an important goal, libraries need to be more proactive in their efforts to train all librarians to be culturally competent. Librarians need to be trained in best practices in serving all communities, not just their own. It may be some time before library schools reform their curriculum to incorporate diversity and multicultural education into their classes to help future librarians develop the foundation needed to work with diverse cultures. It is incumbent on libraries to incorporate diversity training into the work flow of staff. Hiring a designated librarian to promote these efforts is one way to advance these goals. Libraries can also provide mentoring, role models, and internship opportunities for students and librarians of color. They can build strong partnerships with other organizations and work closely with them.

Libraries can play a significant role in library and campus diversity. A designated diversity librarian can coordinate outreach to disadvantaged student populations, assist with recruitment of librarians of color and with diverse student workers, and engage in diversity dialogs at the campus level. A diversity librarian can provide targeted information literacy skills programs, support diversity initiatives on campus, and build and publicize collections that reflect the needed diversity representation and issues. Diversity initiatives should be integrated into the fabric of all library functions, and a diversity librarian can oversee this process. Accomplishing this would get libraries one step closer to the vision of at least one of the interviewees, who said, "One day our profession will mirror what we preach."

CHAPTER TEN

Resources

The resources related to diversity efforts in this chapter are selected resources. The lists are not meant to be exhaustive. In various cases, omissions may occur if information was not readily available or easily found at libraries (such as diversity committees and residency programs). Because these resources are accessible through the Web, the URLs may shift. If that occurs, searching by the title of the resource may reveal the current Web address

Assessment (Diversity)

- ClimateQUAL: Organizational Climate and Diversity Assessment (OCDA). The Organizational Climate and Diversity Assessment is a survey tool first administered in the University of Maryland (UM) Libraries in 2000 as a means of collecting information about staff perceptions about how well the libraries were doing in achieving the climate for diversity and organizational health. This is a Joint Project of the University of Maryland Libraries and Industrial/Organizational Psychology Program and the Association of Research Libraries. ARL's ClimateQUAL website, which contains information about the origins, partners, publications, videos, and FAQs, is at www. climatequal.org/about/news/new_site.shtml. The University of Maryland ClimateQUAL webpage is www.lib.umd.edu/ocda/index.html. For a PowerPoint presentation, see www.arl.org/bm~doc/lowry_baughman.pps.
- *Community Analysis Methods and Evaluative Options: The CAMEO Handbook*: http://skyways.lib.ks.us/pathway/cameo. This handbook provides 12 chapters related to planning, assessing, and analyzing and communicating the results of assessment. Also includes handouts and resources.

- Colorado Department of Education, "Library Services to Diverse and Special Populations: Assess Needs": www.cde.state. co.us/cdelib/diversity/Resources-Assess.htm. Includes examples of collecting community data, internal assessment tools, and additional readings.
- Library Research Service Community Analysis Scan Form, www. lrs.org/public/ca_form.php.
- University of Tennessee Libraries diversity committee's climate survey: www.lib.utk.edu/diversity/activities/staffenrichment/ ClimateSurvey.pdf.

Awards

- Achievement in Library Diversity Research Award. The ALA Office for Diversity annually honors an individual for "Achievement in Library Diversity Research" with a plaque and complimentary annual conference registration: www.ala.org/ala/ aboutala/offices/diversity/divresearchgrants/divresearchhonoree. cfm.
- ALA Annual Diversity Research Grant Program, www.ala.org/ ala/aboutala/offices/diversity/divresearchgrants/diversityresearch. cfm.
- David Cohen/EMIERT Multicultural Award, which encourages and recognizes "articles of significant new research and publication that increases understanding and promotes multiculturalism in libraries in North America": www.ala.org/ ala/mgrps/rts/emiert/emiertawards/cohenaward/cohenaward. cfm.
- GALE/EMIERT Multicultural Award, which recognizes "any significant accomplishments in library services that are national or international in scope and that include improving, spreading, and promoting multicultural librarianship": www.ala.org/ala/ mgrps/rts/emiert/emiertawards/galeaward/galeaward.cfm.

Bibliographies (Online)

- Best Practices for Managing Organizational Diversity. Bibliography of lots of resources with annotations: www.slac. stanford.edu/cgi-wrap/getdoc/slac-pub-12874.pdf.
- Bibliography of Diversity Resources. Compiled by Colorado

State Library (Colorado Department of Education) and the
Colorado Library Advisory Board: http://diversity.aclin.org/
Biblio.cfm.

Books (Selected List)

Adams, Maurianne, Lee Ann Bell, and Pat Griffin. *Teaching for Diversity and Social Justice: A Sourcebook.* New York: Routledge, 1997.

Alire, Camila A., and Orlando Archibeque. *Serving Latino Communities: A How-to-Do-It Manual for Librarians.* New York: Neal-Schuman Publishers, 1998.

American Library Association. *Diversity.* Chicago: American Library Association, 2000.

Avila, Salvador. *Crash Course in Serving Spanish-Speakers.* Westport, CT: Libraries Unlimited, 2008.

Banks, James, and Cherry Banks, eds. *Multicultural Education: Issues and Perspectives,* 5th ed. New York: John Wiley, 2004.

Bosman, Ellen, John P. Bradford, and Robert B. Ridinger. *Gay, Lesbian, Bisexual, and Transgendered Literature: A Genre Guide.* Westport, CT: Libraries Unlimited, 2008.

Cogell, Raquell, and Cindy A. Gruwell. *Diversity in Libraries: Academic Residency.* Westport, CT: Greenwood Press, 2001.

Colorado Council for Library Development. *Diversity Tool Kit.* Denver, CO: External Partnership Subcommittee, Colorado Council for Library Development, Committee on Library Service to Ethnic Populations, 1997.

Constantino, Rebecca. *Literacy, Access, and Libraries among the Language Minority Population.* Lanham, MD: Scarecrow Press, 1998.

Cuban, Sondra. *Serving New Immigrant Communities in The Library.* Westport, CT: Libraries Unlimited, 2007.

Cuesta, Yolanda, and Gail McGovern. *Planning and Marketing Library Services to Culturally Diverse Communities:* [proceedings of an institute held] *July 11–12, 2001.* Memphis, TN: Memphis/Shelby County Public Library and Information Center, 2001.

Curry, Deborah A., and Susan Griswold Blandy. *Racial and Ethnic Diversity in Academic Libraries: Multicultural Issues.* New York: Haworth Press, 1994.

Davis, Kaetrena D. *Global Evolution: A Chronological Annotated Bibliography of International Students in U.S. Academic Libraries.* Chicago:

Association of College and Research Libraries, 2007.

de la Pena McCook, Kathleen, ed. *Ethnic Diversity in Library and Information Science.* Champaign, IL: University of Illinois, Graduate School of Library and Information Science, 2000. Also co-published as a special issue of *Library Trends* 49 (2000): 1–219. Special themed journal.

Dewey, Barbara I., and Loretta Parham. *Achieving Diversity: A How-To-Do-It Manual.* New York: Neal-Schuman Publishers, 2006.

Du Mont, Rosemary Ruhig, Lois Buttlar, and William Caynon. *Multiculturalism in Libraries.* Westport, CT: Greenwood Press, 1994.

Gruwell, Cindy A., and Raquel V. Cogell. *Diversity in Libraries: Academic Residency Programs.* Westport, CT: Greenwood Press, 2001.

Güereña, Salvador. *Library Services to Latinos: An Anthology.* Jefferson, NC: McFarland, 2000.

Güereña, Salvador, ed. *Latino Librarianship: A Handbook for Professionals.* Jefferson, NC: McFarland, 1990.

Hill, Katherine Hoover. *Diversity and Multiculturalism in Libraries.* Greenwich, CT: JAI Press, 1994.

Hills, Gordon H. *Native Libraries: Cross-Cultural Conditions in the Circumpolar Countries.* Lanham, MD: Scarecrow Press, 1997.

Illinois State Library. *Illinois State Library Diversity Program: Diversifying Diversity in Illinois Libraries.* Springfield, IL: Illinois State Library Diversity Program, 2006.

Jones, Plummer Alston. *Still Struggling for Equality: American Public Library Services with Minorities.* Westport, CT: Libraries Unlimited, 2004.

Keller, Shelly G. *Harmony in Diversity: Recommendations for Effective Library Service to Asian Language Speakers.* Sacramento, CA: California State Library, 1998.

Kelsey, Paul, and Sigrid Kelsey. *Outreach Services in Academic and Special Libraries.* Binghamton, NY: Haworth Information Press, 2003.

Kuharets, Irina A., B.A. Cahalan, and F.J. Gitner. *Bridging Cultures: Ethnic Services in the Libraries of New York State.* Albany, NY: New York Library Association Ethnic Services Roundtable, 2001.

Kuharets, Olga R. *Venture into Cultures: A Resource Book of Multicultural Materials and Programs,* 2nd ed. Chicago: American Library Association, 2001.

MacCann, Donnarae, ed. *Social Responsibility in Librarianship: Essays on*

Equality. Jefferson, NC: McFarland, 1989.

Martin, Hillias J., and James R. Murdock. *Serving Lesbian, Gay, Bisexual, Transgender, and Questioning Teens: A How-To-Do-It Manual for Librarians.* New York: Neal-Schuman, 2007.

Martin, Rebecca R. *Libraries and the Changing Face of Academia: Responses to Growing Multicultural Populations.* Metuchen, NJ: Scarecrow Press, 1994.

McCook, Kathleen de la Peña. *Ethnic Diversity in Library and Information Science.* Champaign, IL: University of Illinois, Graduate School of Library and Information Science, 2000.

McCook, Kathleen de la Peña. *Women of Color in Librarianship: An Oral History.* Chicago: American Library Association, 1998.

McCook, Kathleen de la Peña, Kate Lippincott, and Bob Woodard. *Planning for a Diverse Workforce in Library and Information Science Professions.* Tampa, FL: University of South Florida, School of Library and Information Science, Research Group, 1997.

Montiel-Overall, Patricia, and Donald C Adcock. *School Library Services in a Multicultural Society.* Chicago: American Association of School Librarians, 2008.

Muddiman, Dave. *Open to All?: The Public Library and Social Exclusion.* 3 vols. London: Resource: The Council for Museums, Archives and Libraries, 2000.

Neely, Teresa Y. and Khafre K Abif. *In Our Own Voices: The Changing Face of Librarianship.* Lanham, MD: Scarecrow Press, 1996.

Neely, Teresa Y., and Kuang-Hwei Lee-Smeltzer, eds. *Diversity Now: People, Collections, and Services in Academic Libraries.* New York: Haworth Information Press, 2001.

Nicholson, Carol Avery, Ruth Johnson Hill, and Vicente E. Garces. *Celebrating Diversity: A Legacy of Minority Leadership in the American Association of Law Libraries.* Buffalo, NY: William S. Hein & Co., 2006.

Nieto, Sonia. *The Light in Their Eyes: Creating Multicultural Learning Communities.* New York: Teachers College Press, 1999.

Nishii, Lisa H., and Jana L Raver. *Results of the University of Maryland Libraries' Organizational Culture and Diversity Assessment.* College Park, MD: University of Maryland, Industrial/Organizational Psychology Program, 2000.

Osborne, Robin, and Carla D. Hayden, eds. *From Outreach to Equity:*

Innovative Models of Library Policy and Practice. Chicago: American Library Association Office for Literacy and Outreach Services, 2004.

Peterson, Mark F., and Mikael Søndergaard. *Cross Cultural Management.* London: SAGE, 2008.

Peterson, Ray E. *Recruitment and Retention of Minority Personnel and Trustees in Public Libraries.* Denver, CO: The Office, 1996.

Reese, Gregory L., and Ernestine L. Hawkins. *Stop Talking, Start Doing: Attracting People of Color to the Library Profession.* Chicago: American Library Association, 1999.

Riggs, Donald, and Patricia Tarin, eds. *Cultural Diversity in Libraries.* New York: Neal-Schuman, 1994.

Robertson, Deborah A. *Cultural Programming for Libraries' Linking Libraries, Communities and Culture.* Chicago: American Library Association, 2005.

Romain, Joseph, and Mohamed Taher. *Managing Religious Diversity in the Library,* Toronto: Ontario Multifaith Council for Spiritual and Religious Care, 2006.

Ruhig, Rosemary Du Mont, Lois Buttlar, and William Caynon, eds. *Multiculturalism in Libraries,* Westport, CT: Greenwood Press, 1994.

Spectrum Scholarship Program. *Celebrating 10 Years of the Spectrum Scholarship Program.* Chicago: American Library Association, 2007.

Totten, Herman L., and Risa W. Brown. *Culturally Diverse Library Collections for Children.* New York: Neal-Schuman, 1994.

Wheeler, Maurice, ed. *Unfinished Business: Race, Equity, and Diversity in Library and Information Science Education.* Lanham, MD: Scarecrow Press, 2005.

Winston, Mark. *Managing Multiculturalism and Diversity in the Library: Principles and Issues for Administrators.* New York: Haworth Press, 1999.

Wong, Patricia M., Grace Francisco, and Shelly G. Keller. *California Cultural Crossroads.* Sacramento, CA: California State Library, 2007.

Zielinska, Marie F., and Francis T. Kirkwood, eds. *Multicultural Librarianship: An International Handbook.* Munich: K.G. Saur, 1992.

Collection Development
General
- ADL's World of Difference Institute. Multicultural & antibias books for children recommended by the Anti-Defamation

League. This is an annotated list of multicultural and anti-bias children's books, http://childrensbooks.about.com/gi/dynamic/offsite. htm?site=http://www.adl.org/bibliography/default.asp

- American Library Association. Guidelines for the Development and Promotion of Multilingual Collections and Services, revised 2007 by the Library Services to the Spanish-Speaking Committee, Reference User Services Association. http://ala.org/ala/mgrps/divs/rusa/resources/guidelines/guidemultilingual.cfm.
- Cleveland State University, Multicultural Children's Book Database: http://html.ulib.csuohio.edu/bookreviews.
- Database of Award-Winning Children's Literature. Librarian's site where you can search for titles by ethnicity, country, multicultural content, and language: www.dawcl.com/search.asp.
- Develop Collections. Library Services to Diverse and Special Populations. Colorado Department of Education. Includes sample policies, booklists, tips and additional resources for specific populations: www.cde.state.co.us/cdelib/diversity/Resources-Develop.htm.
- Guidelines for the Development and Promotion of Multilingual Collections and Services. RUSA: Reference and User Services Association. Approved January 2007: www.ala.org/ala/mgrps/divs/rusa/resources/guidelines/guidemultilingual.cfm.
- Library and Archives of Canada. "Developing Multicultural Collections," Multicultural Resources and Services Toolkit: www.collectionscanada.gc.ca/multicultural/005007-302-e.html.
- PolyTalk Foreign Language Vendors. Lists vendor contacts for 12+ languages, compiled by Chicago Public Library and part of Illinois library translator network website: www.polytalk.info/resources.html.

African American
- Africa World Press & The Red Sea Press: www.africaworldpressbooks.com/servlet/StoreFront.
- Amistad Press: www.harpercollins.com/imprints/index.aspx?imprintid=518006.
- Black Classic Press: www.blackclassicbooks.com/servlet/

StoreFront.
- Black Studies Collections, Programs, and Web Sites (from the AFAS section): www.afassection.org/blackstudies. html#collections.
- SmileyBooks: http://aalbc.com/writers/smileybooks.htm.
- Third World Press: www.thirdworldpressinc.com.

American Indian
- American Indian Library Association. Book lists, bibliographies, and awards (some info is not updated) for Indian library-related services from this ALA affiliate: http://aila.library.sd.gov.

Book Reviews/Booklists
- ADL's World of Difference Institute. Multicultural & antibias books for children recommended by the Anti-Defamation League. This is an annotated list of multicultural and anti-bias children's books, http://childrensbooks.about.com/gi/dynamic/offsite. htm?site=http://www.adl.org/bibliography/default.asp.
- American Indian Library Association. Book lists, bibliographies, and awards (some info is not updated) for Indian library-related services from this ALA affiliate: http://aila.library.sd.gov.
- Barahona Center for the Study of Books in Spanish for Children and Adolescents. Searchable booklists of Spanish and English books, including bibliographical books, from an academic center that promotes literacy in English and Spanish: www.csusm.edu/ csb.
- Black Issues Book Review. Web site for the magazine: www. bibookreview.com.
- Database of Award-Winning Children's Literature. Librarian's site where you can search for titles by ethnicity, country, multicultural content, and language: www.dawcl.com/search.asp.
- New York Times Book Reviews. Free, registration required. http://topics.nytimes.com/topics/features/books/bookreviews/ index.html.
- QBR: The Black Book Review. www.qbr.com.

Spanish Language

- Barahona Center for the Study of Books in Spanish for Children and Adolescents. Searchable booklists of Spanish and English books, including bibliographical books, from an academic center that promotes literacy in English and Spanish: www.csusm.edu/csb.
- Críticas Magazine. Described on site as "an English speaker's guide to latest Spanish language titles": www.criticasmagazine.com.
- Letras Libras. A Mexican cultural journal, with literature news in English and Spanish: www.letraslibres.com.
- REFORMA Colorado Resources for Librarians: Collection Development. REFORMA-Colorado guidelines for services as well as book and weblinks: http://reformacolorado.org/resources.htm.
- Selecting Spanish-Language Materials for Adults. An excellent PowerPoint summary of the ALA-ASCLA professional development online course from 2006: www.cde.state.co.us/cdelib/download/ppt/ASCLA_SelectingSpanishLanguageMaterials.ppt.
- Serving Diverse Populations: Public Libraries and the Spanish-Speaking Population.
  Basic tenents from this University of Illinois LIS Clips issue are applicable to many diverse populations: http://clips.lis.uiuc.edu/2005_03.html#3.
- Who's Who in U.S. Spanish-Language Publishing. Addressing challenges in developing a collection of Spanish-language books. High Demand, Short Supply, and the Market's Savvy Buyers Managing Spanish-Language Collection Development, by Raya Kuzyk, November 15, 2006.

Conferences/Programs

- American Library Association Diversity & Outreach Fair http://www.ala.org/ala/aboutala/offices/olos/olosprograms/diversityfair/diversityfair.cfm.
- American Library Association Diversity Leadership Institutes. These institutes "examine the concepts of diversity and leadership and provide hands-on techniques and resources

to assist you in furthering diversity in your workplace." from the website: http://www.ala.org/ala/aboutala/offices/diversity/diversityleadership.cfm.

- Association of Research Libraries (ARL) Diversity Programs: www.arl.org/diversity.
- Foro/Transborder Library Forum. Described as "an international border happening/event; where the flow and exchange of ideas and experiences have been taking place alternatively on each side of the border in a systematic and open discourse among librarians discussing binational and trinational border library issues": http://foro.cetys.net/FOROINGLES/index_in.html.
- Joint Librarians of Color Conference. The first conference was held in 2006 in Dallas Texas. See www.ala.org/ala/aboutala/offices/diversity/jclc/jclc2006.cfm For information about the 2012 conference see www.ala.org/ala/aboutala/offices/diversity/jclc/jclc.cfm.
- NAME: National Association of Multicultural Education Conference: http://nameorg.org/conferences.html.
- National Diversity Conference. A forum for sharing information on upcoming diversity and leadership-related conferences and events.www.nationaldiversityconference.com
- National Diversity in Libraries Conference. A biennial conference. Theme and venue change for each conference. For example: "From Groundwork to Action," July 12–14, 2010, Princeton NJ: www.radicalreference.info/diversityconference/2010.
- Texas Diversity and Leadership Conference: www.texasdiversityconference.com.
- Tri-State Diversity Conference (Indiana, Kentucky, Ohio) To network and link resources to help integrate diversity into programs, policies, and practices for creating community well-being: www.ces.purdue.edu/dearborn/diversityconf.htm.

Diversity Committees (ARL Libraries)

The following are examples of academic diversity committee webpages. Most contain diversity action plans, statements, mission, goals, initiatives, meeting minutes, reports, programs, and resources.

- ACRL Racial and Ethnic Diversity Committee: http://ala.org/

ala/mgrps/divs/acrl/about/committees/racialethnic.cfm.

- Indiana University Purdue Library Diversity Council: www.ulib. iupui.edu/about/diversity.
- Kansas University Libraries IS Diversity Committee: Examples of past activities, even though the committee was temporarily in hiatus beginning Dec. 2008. www.lib.ku.edu/diversity.
- Librarians Association of the University of California: Committee on Diversity: www.ucop.edu/lauc/committees/cd/ index.html.
- Michigan State University. Diversity Resources in the MSU Libraries http://guides.lib.msu.edu/page.phtml?page_id=1219.
- Oberlin College Library Diversity Committee: www.oberlin. edu/library/diversity/committee.html.
- Ohio State University Libraries Diversity Committee: http:// library.osu.edu/sites/staff/diversity.
- Ohio University Libraries Diversity Committee: https://www. library.ohiou.edu/coll/diversity/committee.html.
- North Carolina State University Library Diversity: www.lib.ncsu. edu/diversity.
- Penn State University Libraries Diversity Committee: www. libraries.psu.edu/psul/diversity/committee.html.
- Rutgers University Libraries Advisory Committee on Diversity: www.libraries.rutgers.edu/rul/staff/groups/diversity_com/charge. shtml.
- University at Buffalo (New York): www.pss.buffalo.edu/ committees/diversity/diversity.php.
- University of Cincinnati (Ohio) Cultural Diversity Committee: www.libraries.uc.edu/libraries/rwc/faculty/committees/ culturaldiversity.html.
- University of Colorado at Boulder Diversity Committee: http:// ucblibraries.colorado.edu/adminservices/committees.htm.
- University of Connecticut: Diversity at the University of Connecticut Libraries: http://lib.uconn.edu/Diversity.
- University of Illinois at Urbana-Champaign Library Diversity Committee: http://www.library.uiuc.edu/ugl/diversity/ committee.html.
- University of Kentucky Libraries Diversity Committee. Reports available if one searches the library website for "diversity

committee": www.uky.edu/Libraries/index.php.

- University Libraries at Notre Dame Diversity Program: www. library.nd.edu/diversity.
- University of Louisville Libraries: Commitment to Diversity @ Your Library: http://library.louisville.edu/diversity/index.html.
- University of Maryland Libraries Diversity Team: www.lib.umd. edu/groups/diversity.
- University of Michigan: www.lib.umich.edu/library-diversity-committee/about-us.
- University of Minnesota Libraries Diversity Outreach Collaborative: https://wiki.lib.umn.edu/AP/DiversityOutreachC ollaborative?from=AP.DiversityOutreachCommittee.
- University of North Carolina and Greensboro University Libraries: http://s-libweb2.uncg.edu/divres.
- University of Oregon Library Diversity Committee: http:// libweb.uoregon.edu/diversity.
- University of South Florida Diversity Task Force: www.lib.usf. edu/public/index.cfm?Pg=DiversityTaskForce
- University of Tennessee Libraries' Diversity Committee: www. lib.utk.edu/diversity
- University of Washington Libraries Diversity: www.lib. washington.edu/About/diversity.
- Yale University Library Diversity Council: www.library.yale.edu/ lhr/diversity.

E-mail Discussion Lists and Discussion Forums
Many states have their own discussion lists dedicated to library diversity.
- ACRL Racial & Ethnic Diversity Committee.
- http://ala.org/ala/mgrps/divs/acrl/about/committees/racialethnic. cfm#point1
- Mailing List information at: http://lists.ala.org/wws/info/equilibr
- ACRL Residency Interest Group. http://acrl.ala.org/residency. Mailing List information at http://lists.ala.org/wws/info/acrl-rig
- AFAS African American Studies & Librarianship. www. afassection.org/membership.html. The discussion list acrl-afas-l@ ala.org is a forum for topics relating to African American Studies librarianship.
- ALA Ethnic and Multicultural Information Exchange Round

Table. ALA's EMIERT offers a few resources and awards. www.
ala.org/ala/mgrps/rts/emiert/index.cfm.

- Asian Pacific American Librarians Association (APALA). www.
apalaweb.org/publications/apalapub.htm#listserv.
- Association of Research Libraries (ARL) Diversity Program
Minority Librarian Mailing List. To subscribe send a message to
marianne@cni.org.
- Bibliomex—Mexican Librarians Mailing List. http://blogeba.
blogspot.com/2007/09/bibliomex.html To subscribe send
a message to bibliomex-1-request@ccr.dsi.uanl.mx with the
message SUBSCRIBE BIBLIOMEX-L.
- Black Information Professionals' Network is an independent
discussion list dedicated to the concerns and interests of Black
information professionals—librarians, archivists, info brokers,
etc.—and others throughout the African Diaspora with an
interest in the library and information field. To subscribe to
BLACK-IP, send the following command to LISTSERV@
LISTSERV.TEMPLE.EDU. SUBSCRIBE BLACK-IP
yourfirstname yourlastname. The archives are available at: http://
listserv.temple.edu/archives/black-ip.html.
- Chinese American Librarians Association (CALA). To subscribe
send a message to listserv@csd.uwm.edu In the body of your
message type sub CALA your full name.
- Diversity-l@ala.org forum sponsored by ALA's LAMA Diversity
Officers Discussion Group. You do not need to be a member
of LAMA to subscribe to diversity-L. Common topics include
diversity initiatives in libraries, networking, sharing of ideas
to promote diversity. Also noted as the Diversity Officers
Discussion Group. Subscription information at: http://lists.ala.
org/wws/sigrequest/diversity-l.
- Diversity in Academic Libraries: A Facebook group interested
in the advocacy for equality and diversity both within racial and
ethnic communities but also within the library profession. www.
facebook.com/group.php?gid=5380110151.
- Diversity in Academic Libraries (DIAL-South; California).
http://carl-acrl.org/ig/dials.
- Equilibr: discussion of diversity in libraries. This is probably the
broadest and best known professional e-mail discussion list for

reaching a diverse group of librarians. Wide variety of diversity issues in libraries and resources are commonly discussed; job announcements are posted frequently. Subscription address at http://lists.ala.org/wws/info/equilibr

- Ethnic Caucuses. Subscription information at http://lists.ala.org/wws/info/ecaucus.
- Ethnic Materials and Information Exchange Round Table (EMIERT). www.acrl.org/ala/mgrps/rts/emiert/index.cfm.
- FORO/Transborder Libraries Forum. To subscribe send a message to listserv@listserv.arizona.edu. In the body of your message type: sub FORO-L your full name.
- Gay, Lesbian, Bisexual, and Transgender Round Table (GLBRT): http://www.ala.org/ala/mgrps/rts/glbtrt/index.cfm.
- IFLA-L. International Federation of Library Associations mailing list. www.ifla.org/en/mailing-lists. To subscribe, send a message to IFLANET@ifla.org. The IFLA-L archive is browseable from August 1995 to the present and is updated automatically. http://infoserv.inist.fr/wwsympa.fcgi/arc/ifla-l.
- International Librairanship Discussion Groups/Listservs: www.ala.org/ala/aboutala/offices/iro/iroactivities/discussionlists.cfm
- Lezbrian: E-mail discussion list for lesbian librarians and all others interested in relevant resources and issues. http://groups.yahoo.com/group/LEZBRIAN. Subscription address: listserv@listserv.acsu.buffalo.edu. Posting address: lezbrian@listserv.acsu.buffalo.edu.
- Library Services to Non-English Speakers. Information for the ALA Mailing List at: nonenglishspeakers@ala.org
- Middle East Librarians' Association: www.mela.us. See instructions for subscribing to Melanet (www.mela.us/melanet.html) and Mideastcat (www.mela.us/mideastcat.html) lists.
- Multicultural-Resources-L is open to anyone interested in issues relevant to multiculturalism and multilingualism in Canada. http://www.lsoft.com/scripts/wl.exe?SL1=MULTICULTURAL-RESOURCES-L&H=INFOSERV.NLC-BNC.CA .To subscribe, send a message to LISTSERV@infoserv.nlc-bnc.ca with the command SUBSCRIBE MULTICULTURAL-RESOURCES-L.
- Non English Access in Catalogs. http://lists.ala.org/wws/info/nonenglishaccess.

- OLOS—Office of Literacy and Outreach Services: www.ala.org/ala/aboutala/offices/olos/index.cfm.
- Reformanet. REFORMA is the National Association to Promote Library Services to the Spanish Speaking, and Reformanet is the organization's electronic forum. Discussion of Latino library issues, materials, and public service are common threads. This is a closed list. To subscribe follow the instructions at http://reforma.creighton.edu/mailman/listinfo/reformanet.
- SALALM (Seminar on the Acquisition of Latin American Library Materials). To subscribe send a message to listserv@uga.cc.uga.edu. In the body of your message type: sub LALA-L your full name.
- Spectrum Recruitment Committee: http://lists.ala.org/wws/info/specrecruit.
- Spectrum Scholar List: www.ala.org/ala/aboutala/offices/diversity/spectrum/spectrum.cfm. To join the list see information at: http://lists.ala.org/wws/info/scholars.-

Ethnic Caucuses/Interest Groups/Agencies/Round Tables/Committees

Most of these groups are on the national level, so look for regional groups as well.

- Africana Librarians Council: www.library.upenn.edu/collections/africa/ALC.
- Association of College and Research Libraries (ACRL): Racial and Ethnic Diversity Committee: http://ala.org/ala/mgrps/divs/acrl/about/committees/racialethnic.cfm.
- ALA Association of Specialized and Cooperative Library Agencies. ALA's ASCLA links to important issue areas in serving special populations such as prison populations, people with physical challenges, and the elderly: www.ala.org/ala/mgrps/divs/ascla/asclaissues/issues.cfm.
- American Indian Library Association: www.ailanet.org.
- ALA Gay, Lesbian, Bisexual, and Transgendered Round Table. ALA's GLBTRT has a newsletter, booklists, and a discussion list: www.ala.org/ala/mgrps/rts/glbtrt/index.cfm.
- Asian/Pacific American Librarians Association: www.apalaweb.org.

- Black Caucus of ALA: www.bcala.org.
- Chinese American Librarians Association: www.cala-web.org.
- EMIERT (Ethnic and Multicultural Information Exchange Round Table). Serves as a source of information on recommended ethnic collections, services, and programs: www.ala.org/Template.cfm?Section=emiert.
- European Association of Sinological Librarians: www.easl.org.
- Internet Chinese Librarians Club: www.iclc.us.
- Library Services to Multicultural Populations Section (of IFLA—the International Federation of Library Associations and Institutions): www.ifla.org.
- Middle East Librarians' Association: www.mela.us. See instructions for subscribing to Melanet (www.mela.us/melanet.html) and Mideastcat (www.mela.us/mideastcat.html) lists.
- Multicultural Libraries Network: www.openroad.net.au/mcl.
- National Association for Multicultural Education: http://nameorg.org.
- National Center for Cultural Competency: http://www11.georgetown.edu/research/gucchd/nccc.
- National Diversity Council: www.nationaldiversitycouncil.org.
- Office of Women's Affairs Report on the Status of Women: www.indiana.edu/~owa.
- OLC—Ohio Library Council Diversity Awareness and Resource Committee www.olc.org/diversity.
- REFORMA. Promotes library and information services to Latinos and the Spanish speaking. Website describes awards, links resources including WebJunction, mentoring program, Spanish for Librarians document, children's website links, and storytime: www.reforma.org.

Grants/Fellowship/Scholarship Resources

- ALA Awards and Scholarships. A list of state chapters providing awards and scholarships:.http://cro.ala.org/chapters/index.php?title=Awards_and_Scholarships. A browseable list of awards, grants and scholarships is available at http://www.ala.org/template.cfm?template=/CFApps/awards_info/browse.cfm&FilePublishTitle=Awards,%20Grants%20and%20Scholarships&rtype=ALL

- ALA/LAMA—Cultural Diversity Grant. From the webpage (www.ala.org/Template.cfm?Section=lamaawa rds&Template=/ContentManagement/ContentDisplay. cfm&ContentID=11484): "The goals of the grant program are to support the creation and dissemination of resources that will assist library administrators and managers in developing a vision and commitment to diversity, and in fostering and sustaining diversity throughout their institutions; to increase the representation and advancement of people of color in the field of library administration and management and to establish productive partnerships between LAMA and major national organizations representing minority interests; to strengthen the diversity of LAMA membership, committees, and officers and integrate diversity into all aspects of the Association's work."
- ALA Spectrum initiative. www.ala.org/ala/aboutala/offices/ diversity/spectrum/spectrum.cfm.
- Archie Motley Memorial Scholarship for Minority Students. The purpose is to provide financial assistance to minority students pursuing graduate education in archival administration. www. midwestarchives.org/mc/page.do?sitePageId=92950.
- ARL Diversity Scholars Program (Initiative to Recruit a Diverse Workforce). www.arl.org/diversity/init.
- ARL Initiative to Recruit a Diverse Workforce. From the webpage (http://www.arl.org/diversity/init/index.shtml): "The ARL Initiative to Recruit a Diverse Workforce, funded by the Institute of Museum and Library Services and ARL member libraries, offers a stipend of up to $10,000 to attract students from underrepresented groups to careers in academic and research libraries. These stipends can be coupled with any other financial aid to provide an extra incentive for completing library school as well as providing the opportunity to work in an ARL library upon graduation. This initiative reflects the commitment of ARL members to create a diverse academic and research library community that will better meet the new challenges of global competition and changing demographics."
- ARL Residency Position Announcements Database website. http://residencies.arl.org
- Bill Gates Grants. www.gatesfoundation.org/grantseeker/Pages/

funding-united-states-libraries.aspx.

- Diversity Librarians' Network Fellowships: http://
diversitylibrariansnetwork.blogspot.com/2009/07/nlmaahsl-
leadership-fellows-program.html
- Ginny Frankenthaler Memorial Scholarship in Library Science.
From the website: http://selaonline.org/about/scholarships.
htm "The purpose of the scholarship is to recruit beginning
professional librarians who possess potential for leadership and
commitment to service in libraries in the Southeastern United
States. The scholarship provides financial assistance towards
completion of the graduate degree in library science from an
institution accredited by the American Library Association."
- Laura Bush 21st Century Librarian Program. http://www.imls.
gov/applicants/grants/21CenturyLibrarian.shtm. Part of the
Institute of Museum and Library Services.
- Library Services and Technology Act Grants (LSTA)—IMLS.
www.imls.gov/programs/bystate.shtm; www.imls.gov/programs/
programs.shtm.
- LITA/OCLC Minority Scholarship in Library and Information
Technology. www.ala.org/ala/mgrps/divs/lita/litaresources/
litascholarships/litascholarships.cfm#oclc.
- LITA/LSSI Minority Scholarship in Library and Information
Technology. www.ala.org/ala/mgrps/divs/lita/litaresources/
litascholarships/litascholarships.cfm#lssi; www.ala.org/ala/lita/
litaresources/litascholarships/litascholarships.htm#lssi.
- LLAMA: Library and Leadership Management Association
Cultural Diversity Grant. www.ala.org/ala/mgrps/divs/llama/
awards/lamacultural.cfm
- Medical Library Association Grants and Scholarships. From the
web page: http://www.mlanet.org/awards/grants; "MLA offers
a variety of scholarships and grants to assist qualified students
in graduate library science programs and to enable practicing
health sciences librarians to take advantage of opportunities for
continuing professional development."
  – MLA Scholarship for Minority Students. www.mlanet.org/
  awards/grants/minstud.html
  – MLS/NLM Spectrum Scholarship. www.mlanet.org/awards/
  grants/mla_nlmspectrum.html

- Medical Library Education Section of the Medical Library Association. www.mles.mlanet.org/fellows.html.
- National Library of Medicine Associate Fellowship Program. www.nlm.nih.gov/about/training/associate/applicinfo.html.
- OCLC Minority Fellowship Program. This is a one-year full-time appointment. www.oclc.org/careers.
- Reforma Scholarship Program. Open to citizens and permanent residents of the United States who are Spanish speakers. www.reforma.org/scholarship2009.html.
- Prism fellowship at the University of Rhode Island funded by IMLS. From the web site www.uri.edu/artsci/lsc/People/PRISM. html "dedicated to educating future librarians about information literacy for diverse populations."
- Special Library Association Scholarships and Grants. From the website: http://www.sla.org/content/resources/scholargrant/ index.cfm "Each year, SLA awards $30,000 to at least 5 students who have demonstrated their ability and desire to contribute to the Special Librarian field. Details regarding the different scholarships, requirements, instructions and applications are outlined."
  - Affirmative Action Scholarship: www.sla.org/content/resources/ scholargrant/scholar/index.cfm#aascholar
- Sylvia Murphey Williams Fund. The Illinois Library Association hosts a fundraiser (a Diversitea) at each Illinois Library Association Annual Conference to raise money to provide additional scholarship money for students who earn the ALA Spectrum scholarship. http://illinoislibrarydiversity.blogspot. com.

Outreach

- ALA Diversity Fair Abstracts. Links to past presentations at ALA's annual event profiling library practices and programs. www.ala.org/Template.cfm?Section=diversityfair#1.
- ALA Office for Literacy & Outreach Services. Outreach Areas as well as Resources pages for tipsheets on various populations; also links to various ALA associations of color. www.ala.org/ala/ aboutala/offices/olos/index.cfm.
- Diversity@Your Library Toolkit. www.atyourlibrary.nsw.gov.au/

pages/diversity/toolkit.cfm.
- Lincoln Trails Regional Library System Diversity . www.librarydiversity.info.
- Yolanda Cuesta community leader guide. www.webjunction.org/slo-workshop-materials/articles/content/439382.
- Apunte, Jose. Suggested Outreach Activities—Spanish Speakers Grid.http://oregon.4h.oregonstate.edu/oregonoutreach/resources/connectingcommunitiesdocs/SuggestedOutreachActivities.pdf.
- Web Junction. Currently there are sections devoted to people with disabilities, immigrants and world languages, Spanish speakers and tribal and First Nation communities. www.webjunction.org/1 (lots of great examples, plans, exercises); www.webjunction.org/spanish-diversity-training/resources/overview; www.webjunction.org/latino-perceptions/resources/wjarticles.
- International Federation of Library Associations and Institutions (IFLA). Multicultural Communities: Guidelines for Library Service, 2nd ed. IFLA, 1998. http://archive.ifla.org/VII/s32/pub/guide-e.htm.
- Office of Literacy and Outreach. Library outreach to underserved populations. www.ala.org/Template.cfm?Section=Outreach_Resources.

Recruitment

- American Library Association. Recruitment for Diversity. Includes a checklist for constructing the job announcement and for recruiting, as well as other resources. www.ala.org/ala/aboutala/offices/diversity/recruitmentdiversity.cfm.
- ALA's Office for Diversity. www.ala.org/ala/aboutala/offices/diversity/index.cfm.ALA Spectrum Scholarship Program. www.ala.org/ala/aboutala/offices/diversity/spectrum/spectrum.cfm.
- ALA Recruitment for Diversity. Includes resources for recruiting a diverse pool of applicants. http://www.ala.org/ala/aboutala/offices/diversity/recruitmentdiversity.cfm
- California Librarians recruitment project (career opportunities for minorities for librarianship).
- CIRLA Fellows program, Georgetown University Library—

recruiting for diversity: careers in librarianship http://
cirlafellows.georgetown.edu.
- Hiring for Diversity. www.sol-plus.net/plus/todo/hiring.htm.
- Project to Recruit the Next Generation of Librarians. includes
  libraries of Notre Dame, Holy Cross, Indiana University South
  Bend, and Valparaiso. www.library.nd.edu/diversity/summer/
  imls/index.shtml.
- Recruiting for Diversity. Diversity Central: Resources for
  Cultural Diversity at Work. www.diversityhotwire.com/leaders_
  toolkit/toolkit/recruiting1.html.
- Reforma Mentoring Program. Includes goals, objectives,
  timeline, and guidelines and forms. www.reforma.org/
  mentoringprogram.html
- University of Arizona School of Library and Information Science
  Knowledge River Program. http://sirls.arizona.edu/about/
  knowledgeRiverIndex —IMLS funded program that educates
  culturally and linguistically sensitive library and information
  professionals to serve and represent these communities within
  the field.
- University of Minnesota Institute for Early Career Librarians.
  For new librarians from underrepresented groups. www.lib.umn.
  edu/sed/institute.

Residency Programs
- ARL Database of Library Residency and Internship Programs.
  http://careers.arl.org.
- Auburn University. www.lib.auburn.edu/diversity.html.
- Cornell Library Junior Fellows Program, Cornell University
  Library. www.library.cornell.edu/diversity/jrfellows.
- Cornell University Minority Fellowship Program. www.library.
  cornell.edu/Adminops/minority.html.
- Indiana University Library Undergraduate Fellowship (IUPU
  Diversity Fellowship). www.ulib.iupui.edu/about/diversity/
  fellowship.
- Kansas State University post-MLS residency program. www.
  lib.k-state.edu/jobs/#residency
- Kent State University (SLIS) & Ohio State University Libraries
  KSU/OSUL Diversity Student Fellowship. www.lib.ohio-state.

edu/Lib_Info/diversfellow.html

- Georgetown University Law Library Residency Program. http://www.ll.georgetown.edu/staff/resident/index.cfm
- McIntyre Library Diversity Internship. University of Wisconsin—Eau Claire Library Diversity Internship.
- National Library of Medicine Associate Fellowship Program. www.nlm.nih.gov/about/training/associate/index.html
- North Carolina State University Fellows. www.lib.ncsu.edu/fellows.
- Ohio State University Libraries. Mary P. Key Diversity Residency Program. http://library.osu.edu/sites/staff/diversity/residency.php
- Purdue University Libraries Diversity Residency Program www.lib.purdue.edu/diversity/residency08.html
- Syracuse University Library Resident Librarians. http://library.syr.edu/blog/news/archives/001642.php
- University of Arkansas Librarian-In-Residence Program. http://libinfo.uark.edu/diversity/residency/overview.asp
- University of Buffalo: The State University of New York Library Internship/Residency Program. http://ublib.buffalo.edu/libraries/residency/index.html
- University of Delaware Library. Pauline A. Young Residency http://www2.lib.udel.edu/personnel/residency/index.html.
- University of Iowa Librarian Residency Program. www.lib.uiowa.edu/about/employment/residency.html
- University of Minnesota Libraries, Residency Program. https://wiki.lib.umn.edu/ResidentLibrarian/HomePage
- University of New Mexico Libraries Resident Program. http://elibrary.unm.edu/residentprogram/
- University of North Carolina Greensboro. The UNCG University Libraries have established a two-year diversity residency. http://library.uncg.edu/divres/program.
- University of Notre Dame Librarian-in-Residence Program. www.library.nd.edu/diversity/residence.shtml.
- University of Notre Dame Summer Diversity Program, University Libraries, www.library.nd.edu/diversity/summer/index.shtml.
- University of Pittsburgh University Library System/DLIS Minority Fellowship Program. www.sis.pitt.edu/~dlis/academics/

download/UlsSisMinApp.pdf.
- University of Pittsburgh Spectrum Doctoral Fellowships (partnering with ALA, the Institute of Museum and Library Services and the School of Information Science at the University of Pittsburgh. www.ala.org/ala/aboutala/offices/diversity/spectrum/phdfellowship/phd.cfm
- University of Tennessee Libraries Diversity Residency Program. www.lib.utk.edu/diversity/activities/residency/index.html..

Retention
- ACRL wiki. Working with and Retaining New Librarians. http://wikis.ala.org/acrl/index.php/Working_with_and_Retaining_New_Librarians.
- Retention for Diversity. Diversity Central: Resources for Cultural Diversity at Work. www.diversityhotwire.com/leaders_toolkit/toolkit/retention1.html.

Selected Libraries
- Diversity Exchange (programming ideas) http://theoceancountylibrary.org/About/recipe_cards.pdf; http://theoceancountylibrary.org/About/Diversity-Plan.htm.
- Enoch Pratt Free Library, www.prattlibrary.org.
- Hennepin County Library. Immigrant resources: www.hclib.org/newimmigrants; assistive technology: www.hclib.org/pub/info/Accessibility.cfm; events, resources and new titles in Spanish:www.hclib.org/pub/info/welcome/index.cfm?language=Spanish&div=material.
- Indiana University Northwest Library Diversity Resources: www.iun.edu/~lib/diversity/
- Librarians Association of the University of California: Resources on Diversity Database. http://internal.library.ucsc.edu/comm/lauc/diversity.
- Ohio State University—Diversity. www.osu.edu/diversity.
- Penn State Diversity in Libraries—Examples and Resources. www.libraries.psu.edu/psul/diversity/resources/diversitylinks.html.
- Queens Borough Public Library. Web-Based—Multicultural Resources, including links to Hispanic web sites (bilingual and

in Spanish). www.queenslibrary.org/index.aspx?page_nm=NAP_
MulticulturalResources

- San José Public Libraries and San José State University Library.
  Paths to Lifelong Learning: www.sjlibrary.org/gateways/index.
  htm; Multicultural Gateway: www.sjlibrary.org/gateways/
  multicultural/index.htm.
- UIUC Diversity and Multicultural Information. www.library.
  uiuc.edu/ugl/diversity/library.html.
- University of Illinois at Urbana-Champaign: Diversity and
  Multicultural Information. www.library.uiuc.edu/ugl/diversity.
- University of Oregon—Diversity. http://diversity.uoregon.edu/
  main.htm.
- University of Tennessee–Knoxville Libraries Diversity
  Committee. Diversity definition and activities to support the
  university's diversity plan; events and links to library diversity.
  www.lib.utk.edu/diversity.
- University of Wisconsin–Milwaukee: Multicultural Services
  Librarian Page www.uwm.edu/Libraries/multicultural.

Social Networking Resources
Blogs
- ACRL Residency Interest Group. http://acrl.ala.org/residency/
- BlogJunction, Spanish Outreach: http://blog.webjunctionworks.
  org/index.php/category/spanish-outreach.
- Diversity Librarians' Network: http://diversitylibrariansnetwork.
  blogspot.com.
- Filipino Librarian Blog: http://filipinolibrarian.blogspot.com.
- Illinois Cultural and Racial Diversity Committee Blog: www.
  illinoislibrarydiversity.blogspot.com.
- New York Public Library Diversity Blog: www.nypl.org/blogs/
  subject/diversity.
- UM Library Diversity on Twitter: http://twitter.com/um_ldc.
- Web Junction http://wikis.ala.org/diversity/index.php/Main_Page
- Who's News? Diversity Every Day Blog, by SPJ (Society of
  Professional Journalists): http://blogs.spjnetwork.org/diversity.

Facebook
- ACRL Residency Interest Group: http://www.facebook.com/

pages/ACRL-Residency-Interest-Group/113621396297?v=info.
- Academic Library Fellows and Residents: A group for past and present participants of academic library residency and fellowship programs, but also welcoming to those with an interest in these program. www.facebook.com/group.php?gid=2330389721.
- Dial-South (Diversity in Academic Libraries). An interest group of California Academic Research Libraires. http://www.facebook.com/group.php?gid=5380110151.
- Emiert (Ethnic and Multicultural Exchange Round Table: http://www.facebook.com/group.php?gid=4228493543.
- Reforma: A group for individuals interested in services for the Spanish-Speaking www.new.facebook.com/pages/REFORMA/26439643928.
- Spectrum Scholar Program: www.facebook.com/pages/Spectrum-Scholarship-Program/96326213617.

Wikis
- American Library Association—Diversity. http://wikis.ala.org/diversity/index.php/Main_Page.
- ALA Diversity directory http://wikis.ala.org/diversity/index.php/Diversity_Directory (table of content for the wiki)
- Diversity connects–Colorado Library Diversity Summit Wiki. http://diversityconnects.wetpaint.com/?t=anon.
- Diversity in the Workplace: ALA wiki (training programs, resources). http://wikis.ala.org/professionaltips/index.php/Diversity_in_the_Workplace.
- NMRLS Diversity Wiki. http://nmrls-diversity-services.pbwiki.com/FrontPage?lo=473b13ec.
- Reforma wiki. http://reformaknowledge.wetpaint.com/?t=anon.
- Serving Multicultural Populations: ALA wiki. http://wikis.ala.org/professionaltips/index.php/Serving_Multicultural_Populations.
- Spectrum Wiki: ALA wiki. http://wikis.ala.org/spectrum/index.php/Main_Page.

Training/Staff Development
- Bendick Jr., M., M. L. Egan, and S. M. Lofhjelm. (2001). Workforce diversity training: From anti-discrimination

compliance to organizational development. Human Resource Planning 24, no. 2 (2001): 10–26.

- Diversity Appreciation, Training and Management. Developed by Free Management Library. Includes overviews and sections on major topics, teaching diversity appreciation and management and valuing diversity. www.managementhelp.org/emp_well/diversty/diversty.htm
- Training for Diversity. Diversity Central: Resources for Cultural Diversity at Work. www.diversityhotwire.com/leaders_toolkit/toolkit/training1.html.
- Web Junction. Currently there are sections devoted to people with disabilities, immigrants and world languages, Spanish speakers. and tribal and First Nation communities. www.webjunction.org/populations-served.

Websites
General Diversity Sites/Resources
- American Institute for Managing Diversity. www.aimd.org.
- American Library Association Office for Diversity. Includes the mission, initiatives and projects, member groups, events, and popular resources. www.ala.org/ala/aboutala/offices/diversity/index.cfm.
- Anti-Defamation League. www.adl.org.
- Association of American Colleges and Universities Diversity Web. www.diversityweb.org.
- Background on Multicultural and Diversity Topics. http://ala.org/ala/mgrps/divs/acrl/about/committees/racialethnic.cfm#point3.
- Center for Research on Education, Diversity, and Excellence, University of California, Berkeley. http://crede.berkeley.edu.
- CSLP summer library program diversity. Many resources for disabilities. www.cslpreads.org/overview.html.
- Cultural Events Calendar. Compiled by Colorado State Library (Colorado Department of Education) and the Colorado Library Advisory Board. Highlights and describes cultural events, holidays, and the birthdays of notable persons of various backgrounds. http://diversity.aclin.org/EDTKCalendar.cfm. See also the Multicultural Calendar at www.dom.com/about/

education/culture/index.jsp
- Diversity Tool Kit. http://diversity.aclin.org.
- Diversity and Libraries: Providing Information to Empower Multicultural Communities. http://polaris.gseis.ucla.edu/cchu/diversity/Index.html.
- Diversity Appreciation, Training and Management. www.mapnp.org/library/emp_well/diversty/diversty.htm.
- Diversity Hub: An Interactive Resource Hub for Higher Education. Includes conferences, papers, position openings, innovations, research and trends. www.diversityweb.org.
- Diversity Training University International. www.dtui.com.
- National Center for Cultural Competency. http://www11.georgetown.edu/research/gucchd/NCCC/foundations/frameworks.html.
- Ocean County Library's Diversity Database. The database is browseable and searchable by community, age group, and difficulty. Others can contribute programs to the database as well. http://diversity.theoceancountylibrary.org.
- Office of Minorities in Higher Education, American Council on Education. www.acenet.edu/AM/Template.cfm?Section=CAREE&Template=/TaggedPage/TaggedPageDisplay.cfm&TPLID=58&ContentID=20366.
- OLC Diversity Awareness and Resources Committee. www.olc.org/diversity.
- Teaching Tolerance (Southern Poverty Law Center). www.tolerance.org.
- Web Junction. www.webjunction.org/1 (lots of great examples, plans, exercises); www.webjunction.org/spanish-diversity-training/resources/overview; www.webjunction.org/latino-perceptions/resources/wjarticles.

National/International
- ACRL: Racial and Ethnic Diversity Committee. http://ala.org/ala/mgrps/divs/acrl/about/committees/racialethnic.cfm.
- ALA Office of Diversity. As one of the many offices within ALA, the Office for Diversity serves as the liaison to the Committee on Diversity and its subcommittees. Additionally, this office administers Spectrum, a scholarship program designed to

improve library service through the development of an ethnically diverse workforce. It provides a clearinghouse for diversity resources. It provides resources on diversity issues, including creating a diversity action and inclusion plan, diversity climate surveys, recruitment, and retention and training. http://www.ala. org/ala/aboutala/offices/diversity/index.cfm.

- ALA Diversity website: www.ala.org/ala/diversity/diversity.html
- ALA Diversity Directory wiki. http://wikis.ala.org/diversity/ index.php/Diversity_Directory.
- ALA Diversity Online (Library Specific Web Resources for Serving Underrepresented Populations with links to key sources and articles for various special populations as well as general diversity resources). www.ala.org/ala/aboutala/offices/diversity/ archive/diversityonline/diversityonline.cfm.
- ALA Office for Literacy and Outreach Services (See Outreach Areas as well as Resources pages for tipsheets on various populations; also links to various ALA associations of color). www.ala.org/ala/aboutala/offices/olos/index.cfm.
- ARL Diversity Programs—Association of Research Libraries. www.arl.org/diversity.
- ARL Programs/Projects. www.ala.org/ala/aboutala/offices/ diversity/index.cfm.
- Canada. Library and Archives Canada. Multicultural Resources and Services Toolkit. www.collectionscanada.gc.ca/ multicultural/005007-301-e.html.
- Colorado Department of Education: Library Services to Diverse and Special Populations. Includes diversity plans, assessment, collections, programs, leaders in diversity. www.cde.state.co.us/ cdelib/librarydiversity.htm.
- IFLANET Library Services to Multicultural Populations Committee. www.ifla.org/en/mcultp.
- Lincoln Trails Regional Library System Diversity. www. librarydiversity.info
- Multicultural Center Prague. www.mkc.cz/en/libraries-for-all.html.
- Ohio Library Council Diversity Awareness and Resources Committee. www.olc.org/diversity/best_prac.html.

Appendix A
Survey Questions—
Multicultural Librarians

Instructions: Please choose the appropriate responses below. This survey should take about 10–15 minutes to complete. Thank you for your honesty and time.

Part I. Library School Information

1. From which library school did you obtain your degree?
   <write-in box>
2. What year did you get your Library degree?
   <write-in box>
3. Did you specifically choose this library school based on courses offered that you thought would be relevant to a career working with diverse cultures?¨
   ☐ Yes
   ☐ No, I hadn't entered library school thinking about working with diverse populations
   ☐ No, I chose this library school for other reasons.
   ☐ Please specify (check here)
   <write-in box>
4. Do you feel that your library school program prepared you for working with multiple cultures?
   ☐ Yes
   ☐ Somewhat
   ☐ No
5. Did your library school offer a specific course related to multicultural librarianship?
   ☐ Yes
   ☐ No
6. If library schools were to offer multicultural librarianship as part of their curriculum how should it be offered?
   ☐ Required

☐ An elective
☐ Elements of working with diverse cultures interspersed into every course

7. How many courses did you take as an undergraduate where the primary focus was on ethnic diversity?

<write-in box>

8. Was there anything in your graduate education at the library school that directed you to pursue a job as multicultural librarian?
☐ Yes, very motivating faculty and/or courses
☐ Not particularly—I was already interested in this field.
☐ No, I hadn't really thought of it.
☐ If so, what? (please check box)

<write-in box>

Part II. Current Position Information

9. What is your current job title? <drop-down list>
☐ Diversity Librarian
☐ Diversity officer
☐ Diversity coordinator
☐ Ethnic Studies and Multicultural Librarian
☐ Multicultural librarian
☐ Multicultural Services Librarian
☐ Outreach Librarian for Multicultural Services
☐ Other please specify

<write-in box>

10. How long have you been in this position? <drop-down list>
☐ Less than a year
☐ 1–3 years
☐ 4–9 years
☐ 10–15 years
☐ More than 15 years

11. Was this advertised as an entry level position?
☐ Yes
☐ No
☐ It was open to junior and senior librarians

Part III. The Hiring Process

12. Did you intentionally seek a position that was dedicated to

multicultural/diversity services? In other words—was this the job you left library school hoping to pursue or after working in libraries wanted to devote your energies to this type of position?

- ☐ Yes
- ☐ No
- ☐ Comment

<write-in box>

13. What was the main reason you applied to the position you now have? <drop-down list>

- ☐ Job responsibilities
- ☐ Institutional reputation
- ☐ Location
- ☐ Cast a wide net
- ☐ Other—please specify

14. Had there been a previous person in the position?

- ☐ Yes
- ☐ No

15. Do you feel that the sentiment was that the person in this position should be from an ethnic or underrepresented group?

- ☐ Yes
- ☐ No
- ☐ Comment

<write-in box>

16. Do you feel that it is necessary for someone in this position to be of a group outside of the dominant culture (someone who is not of White European American origin and a native English speaker?)

- ☐ Yes
- ☐ No
- ☐ Comment

<write-in box>

17. Did you feel that your cultural/ethnic background had an impact on the interview process (positive or negative)?

- ☐ Yes
- ☐ No
- ☐ Comment

<write-in box>

18. Was the search committee expecting someone to come in who had already established multicultural services elsewhere?

☐ Yes

☐ No

☐ Don't know

19. Did you find that you had to be creative in trying to fit your experiences into what was envisioned for this job?

☐ Yes, although I had bits and pieces of what was requested for this job, I had to paint the picture of how that could fit in at this institution

☐ No. I had already done similar work so I could simply share the experiences

☐ Other—please specify

<write-in box>

20. Did you believe that you had all of the qualifications, skills, and experiences that were asked for in this position?

☐ Yes

☐ Not really, but I was able to show how what I had could be valuable.

☐ Other—Please explain

<write-in box>

21. Did you find it difficult to find relevant examples elsewhere of accomplishments, plans, programs of multicultural/diversity librarians?

☐ Yes

☐ No

☐ Comment

<write-in box>

22. What made you the most qualified for this job?

☐ Experience working with diverse cultures

☐ From an ethnic group

☐ Very outgoing and make connections easily

☐ Public relations and marketing abilities

☐ Other

<write-in box>

23. Why do you think that it may be difficult to get a large pool of candidates to apply to a posting of a multicultural/diversity librarian?

☐ Not many minority librarians available (if that's what the search committee was looking for)

☐ The position carries some negative connotations with it for some (one person to do it all, hard to establish a program, isolation…)

☐ Not a position that one learns about in library school and not many examples to inspire librarians to pursue this

☐ Librarians who are white and English speaking might feel that they won't be considered for this so they overlook it.

☐ Other—please specify

<write-in box>

Part IV. Reality of the Job

24. Do you feel that the expectations of the job are realistic and manageable?

☐ Yes

☐ No

☐ Comment

<write-in box>

25. If no, please choose reasons.

☐ I have too many other job responsibilities and can't devote the time I need to accomplish my primary goals and objectives.

☐ It's difficult to get others to work with me on developing and initiating programming.

☐ People don't seem to understand the need for this position.

☐ Other—please specify

<write-in box>

26. Who did you turn to for guidance on this job?

☐ colleague at work

☐ mentor at work

☐ no one- I just went it alone

☐ library listservs/discussion groups related to this position

☐ books

☐ articles

☐ Other—please specify

<write-in box>

27. Which was the first item in the list below that you addressed when you took the job?

☐ establishing relationships and identifying groups to partner with (learning the culture of the institution and the constituencies that I would work with.)

☐ becoming a presence in the library and the community through participation on committees, training, workshops and participation at events

☐ developing a plan of action and getting the support needed to proceed.

☐ developing a library environment that embraces diversity

☐ Other—please specify

<write-in box>

28. Which of the following has/have been the most challenging aspect(s) of the job?

☐ establishing relationships and identifying groups to partner with (learning the culture of the institution and the constituencies that I would work with.)

☐ becoming a presence in the library and the community through participation on committees, training, workshops and participation at events

☐ developing a plan of action and getting the support needed to proceed.

☐ developing a library environment that embraces diversity

☐ Other—please specify

<write-in box>

29. What is the greatest challenge that you find working with groups from various cultures (ethnic, racial, linguistic, religious…?)

☐ Communication

☐ Understanding cultural nuances

☐ Socially acceptable norms

☐ Approachability

☐ Gaining an entree (being accepted)

☐ Other—please specify

<write-in box>

Part IV. Job Satisfaction

30. Job Satisfaction: Are you satisfied with your job?

☐ Yes

☐ No

☐ Sometimes (there are positive and negative elements)

31. Do you feel that your department contributes positively to your growth?

☐ Yes—they are supportive, listen to my ideas and are helpful in the execution of the ideas

☐ Not as much as I would like—please explain

Indicate your satisfaction with each of the following aspects of your current position by checking the most correct response.

	Very satisfied	Mostly satisfied	Somewhat satisfied	Somewhat dissatisfied	Dissatisfied	N/A
32. Autonomy on the job (able to operate independently)						
33. Work assignment and workload						
34. Interaction with peers						
35. Opportunities for professional development						
36. Proportion of faculty of ethnic descent in the library						

To what extent do you feel…

	To a high degree	Moderately	Little	Not at all	No Opinion
37. That there is respect for your knowledge?					
38. Isolated in your workplace?					
39. Unsupported at work?					
40. That you must try to fit into your work environment?					
41. That you have experienced incidences of racial discrimination in the workplace (either towards you or another)?					
42. That your library administration has a high degree of commitment to diversity?					

43. Please indicate the type of library where you currently work.
    <drop-down list>
    ☐ Academic
    ☐ Public
    ☐ Special
    ☐ School
    ☐ Other—please specify
<write-in box>

44. What is your main subject expertise (from a bachelor or other degree, such as Psychology, Education, Music, Physics…)?
<write-in box>

45. Why did you choose to pursue a position as a multicultural/diversity librarian?
    ☐ Previous outreach experience
    ☐ Previous experience working with diverse cultures
    ☐ I hadn't intended to pursue a position such as this but the job was available and it caught my attention.
    ☐ I was inspired by another librarian in a similar position
    ☐ Other—please specify
<write-in box>

Part V. Background Information

46. Please choose one of the following:
    ☐ Male
    ☐ Female
    ☐ Transgender

47. Age Range <drop-down list>
    ☐ Under 25
    ☐ 25–35
    ☐ 35–44
    ☐ 45–54
    ☐ Over 55

48. With which group do you most closely identify?
    ☐ White/Caucasian/European American
    ☐ African American
    ☐ Asian American
    ☐ Native American

☐ Hispanic American
☐ Other—please specify
<write-in box>

49. Are you a Native of the United States?
    ☐ Yes
    ☐ No

50. Was English your childhood language (native language)?
    ☐ Yes
    ☐ No
    ☐ I'm completely bilingual and English was one of my childhood languages
    ☐ Other

51. What other languages can you converse in fluently?
    <write-in box>

52. What other comments do you have about the process of becoming a librarian responsible for coordinating multicultural services (education, job hunting, the job itself)?
    <write-in box>

If you would be willing to send a copy of your job description; be willing to provide a phone interview; or be a contributor to a book chapter on this topic please e-mail me at lmestre@uiuc.edu. Please do not put your email address on the survey itself (in order to protect the confidentiality of your responses). This survey will remain anonymous and in no way connected to any e-mail that you send.

Thank you so much for your assistance.

53. Comments
    <write-in box>

Appendix B
Survey to Library School Administrators

Instructions: Please choose the appropriate responses below. This survey should take about 10–15 minutes to complete. Thank you for your honesty and time.

1. What is your current job title and institution?

<write-in box>

2. How long have you been at this institution?
    - ☐ 1–3 years
    - ☐ 4–7 years
    - ☐ 8–10 years
    - ☐ more than 10 years

3. Does your school/college have a mission statement/strategic plan that specifically mentions the need to teach components of how to work with diverse populations, such as: developing skills in cultural competency; or planning, implementing, and evaluating programs for addressing the information needs of multicultural, multiethnic, and/or multilingual communities?
    - ☐ Yes, we do
    - ☐ We are in the process of including something similar in our mission statement or strategic plan
    - ☐ Not currently
    - ☐ Other

<write-in box>

4. Do you have any faculty with specific background/education in multicultural education/librarianship?
    - ☐ Yes, we have at least one faculty member with expertise in the area.
    - ☐ No, but we do have at least one faculty member with a strong interest in promoting multiculturalism
    - ☐ Not to my knowledge

☐ Other

<write-in box>

5. Does your school have any faculty whose primary research interest intersects with multiculturalism?

☐ Yes

☐ No, not as their primary interest, but there are faculty whose secondary interest is related.

☐ No, not that I'm aware of

☐ Comments

<write-in box>

6. Does this library school offer a specific course in multicultural librarianship (or something similar)? If so, please provide the name.

☐ Yes

☐ No

☐ Course title(s):

<write-in box>

7. If your school does have courses geared to working with diverse populations please list them or provide links to syllabi, if possible.

<write-in box>

8. If your school has a course in multicultural librarianship please check the areas that it covers.

☐ Organization and management of multicultural services/ programs

☐ Impact of technology on the delivery of multicultural services

☐ The library in the multicultural community

☐ Staff training and library orientation programs

☐ Understanding, appreciating and working with other cultures

☐ Methods of research in comparative and ethnographic studies

☐ Cross cultural communication

☐ Collection Development, acquisitions, and cataloging

☐ Recruiting, mentoring, and managing a diverse staff

☐ Resources on multiculturalism

☐ N/A

☐ Other

<write-in box>

9. Is this school in the process of adding a new course for multicultural/diversity librarianship? If so, please provide the title.

☐ yes

☐ no
☐ Course title(s):

<write-in box>

10. Are there components of multicultural/diversity education
     typically included in courses? In other words, are faculty requested/
     required to include information/strategies/information on how to
     work with/provide library services to diverse populations in their
     courses?

     ☐ Yes, faculty make a conscious effort to include those aspects in
         every course
     ☐ Faculty are not required to include those components, but
         many do
     ☐ Faculty are not required to include components and it is not
         known how many do include those components
     ☐ N/A
     ☐ Other

<write-in box>

11. If your school offers some components of multiculturalism in
     courses, are those inclusions formalized (part of the structure of the
     course) or dependent upon the faculty member?

     ☐ There are some courses where at least a section is always offered
         related to multiculturalism
     ☐ Inclusion of multiculturalism is dependent upon the faculty
         member offering the course
     ☐ N/A
     ☐ Other

<write-in box>

12. Has your school considered making a course in multicultural
     librarianship a required course? Please specify why or why not.

<write-in box>

13. What are some ways that students are prepared to provide services
     to a linguistically and culturally diverse population?

     ☐ Specific courses geared to multicultural librarianship
     ☐ Components in courses with aspects of multicultural
         librarianship
     ☐ Workshops or training sessions offered by the school on topics
         related to multiculturalism
     ☐ Only through other courses/workshops offered on campus

☐ Internship/teaching/graduate assistanceship in a library working with someone responsible for multicultural services

☐ Creation of independent study classes to allow the exploration of multicultural librarianship

☐ Other

<write-in box>

14. Are you aware of any graduates of your school who now hold positions as multicultural/diversity librarians?

☐ Yes, we have had graduates who now hold such a title.

☐ We have graduates who work with multicultural services as part of their job, but not as their main role.

☐ No, I'm not aware of any.

☐ Other

<write-in box>

15. If students have expressed desires for programs/courses in multicultural librarianship or outreach, what specific areas have they identified?

<write-in box>

16. What other comments do you have about preparing future librarians to work in a multicultural society and/or working as a multicultural/diversity/outreach librarian?

<write-in box>

Thank you for your time. If you would be willing to send syllabi of courses or other documents (strategic plan, mission statements) including components of multiculturalism please send them to lmestre@uiuc.edu. Thank you.

If you would be willing to provide a short follow-up phone interview, please contact me at: lmestre@uiuc.edu

Thank you again.

Appendix C
Interview Questions

Possible Interview Questions:

1. How did you get interested in multicultural librarianship?
2. How did you get interested in working with diverse cultures?
3. Please share how your library school prepared you for your current position.
4. What do you wish would have been covered in library school that wasn't (pertaining to being successful in this role)?
5. What was it like interviewing for this position? Please share your preparations, expectations, search committee experiences…
6. What have been the most challenging aspects of this job?
7. What have been the most rewarding aspects of this job?
8. What qualifications do you feel someone in this position needs in order to be successful?
9. Do you feel that it is critical to have someone in this position who is from a cultural or ethnic minority group?
10. If someone who was not from a cultural or ethnic minority group were in this position, what advice would you give them for "becoming an ally" and connecting?
11. In general, what advice would you give librarians beginning in this type of position?
12. What would you like the library administration to know about this position?
13. How do you feel this type of position differs from others (such as a reference position or cataloging position) as far as expectations, support…
14. What other comments would you like to share?

Lori Mestre

Appendix D
Online Survey Informed Consent

Survey about Multicultural Librarianship

This survey is being sent to selected individuals via e-mail. This e-mail invites you to participate in the survey.

FOR QUESTIONS ABOUT THE STUDY CONTACT: Lori Mestre, Digital Learning Librarian and Associate Professor of Library Administration University of Illinois at Urbana-Champaign, 426 Main Library, MC-522, 1408 W. Gregory Drive, University of Illinois at Urbana-Champaign, Urbana, Illinois 61801: Telephone: 217-244-4171.

DESCRIPTION: You are invited to participate in a research study on positions with titles related to multicultural/diversity librarians in U.S. libraries. You will be asked to complete an online survey with questions about your position including library school training, hiring practices and job satisfaction. After submitting the survey, you may provide your contact information, by a separate e-mail, if you wish to be contacted for participation in a possible follow-up interview. Your email and contact information will not be connected to your survey data. Your survey responses will remain anonymous.

Any and all information that is received will be kept strictly confidential and will only be seen by authorized individuals connected with this research. Data gathered from the survey will be summarized in the aggregate, excluding all references to individual responses. The aggregated results of the research will be shared with individuals interested in multicultural librarianship, including possible publications and presentations.

RISKS AND BENEFITS: The risks associated with this study are minimal. The risk relates to providing some information that is evaluative in nature of their library administration or work environment. However, the risk is minimal because the survey is intended to be anonymous and you can choose not to answer questions. The benefits which may reasonably be expected to result from this study are improving training, preparation and support for librarians with roles serving diverse populations. I cannot and do not guarantee or promise that you will receive any benefits from this study.

TIME INVOLVEMENT: Your participation in this survey will take approximately 10–15 minutes.

PAYMENTS: You will receive no payment for your participation.

SUBJECT'S RIGHTS: If you have read this form and have decided to participate in this project, please understand your participation is voluntary and you have the right to withdraw your consent or discontinue participation at any time without penalty or loss of benefits to which you are otherwise entitled. Likewise, you have the right to refuse to answer particular questions. Your individual privacy will be maintained in all published and written data resulting from the study.

CONTACT INFORMATION:
- Questions, Concerns, or Complaints: If you have any questions, concerns or complaints about this research study, its procedures, risks and benefits, or alternative courses of treatment, you should contact the Project Investigator: Professor Lori Mestre, 217-365-9994, lmestre@uiuc.edu.
- Independent of the Project Investigator Contact: For information about the rights of human subjects in UIUC-approved research please contact the University of Illinois Institutional Review Board Office (IRB) to speak to an informed individual who is independent of the researcher at (217)-333-0405; irb@uiuc.edu. Persons may call collect if they identify themselves as research subjects. Or write the University of Illinois IRB, Suite 203, MC-419, 528 East Green Street, University of Illinois at Urbana-Champaign, 61801.

I agree to participate in this study and would like to continue. Please click on the survey link below to provide consent and access the survey [https://webtools.uiuc.edu/survey/Secure?id=5207405]

This informed consent statement has been approved by the University of Illinois.

You are encouraged to print a copy of this statement for your records.

Appendix E
Interview Consent Form

A Study about Multicultural Librarianship
FOR QUESTIONS ABOUT THE STUDY CONTACT: Lori Mestre, Digital Learning Librarian and Associate Professor of Library Administration University of Illinois at Urbana-Champaign, 426 Main Library, MC-522, 1408 W. Gregory Drive, University of Illinois at Urbana-Champaign, Urbana, Illinois 61801: Telephone: 217-244-4171. E-mail lmestre@uiuc.edu

DESCRIPTION: You are invited to participate in a research study about multicultural/diversity librarians in U.S. libraries. You will be interviewed about your position including training, hiring practices and job satisfaction. The interview data will be coded immediately after the interview to remove any identifying information and the identifiers will be destroyed. Please be assured that the contact information and data will remain strictly confidential and will be used for research purposes only (including possible publications and presentations).

RISKS AND BENEFITS: There are expected to be no risks to participation in the interview beyond those that exist in everyday life The benefits which may reasonably be expected to result from this study are improving training, preparation and support for librarians with roles serving diverse populations. I cannot and do not guarantee or promise that you will receive any benefits from this study.

TIME INVOLVEMENT: Your participation in this interview will take approximately 15–30 minutes, but can take as long as you desire.

PAYMENTS: You will receive no payment for your participation.

SUBJECT'S RIGHTS: If you have read this form and have decided to participate in this project, please understand your participation is voluntary and you have the right to withdraw your consent or discontinue participation at any time without penalty or loss of benefits to which you are otherwise entitled. Likewise, you have the right to refuse to answer particular questions. Your individual privacy will be maintained in all published and written data resulting from the study.

CONTACT INFORMATION:
- Questions, Concerns, or Complaints: If you have any questions, concerns or complaints about this research study, its procedures, risks and benefits, or alternative courses of treatment, you should contact the Project Investigator: Professor Lori Mestre, 217-365-9994, lmestre@uiuc.edu.
- Independent of the Project Investigator Contact: For information about the rights of human subjects in UIUC-approved research please contact the University of Illinois Institutional Review Board Office (IRB) to speak to an informed individual who is independent of the researcher at (217)-333-0405; irb@uiuc.edu. Persons may call collect if they identify themselves as research subjects. Or write the University of Illinois IRB, Suite 203, MC-419, 528 East Green Street, University of Illinois at Urbana-Champaign, 61801.

I agree to participate in this study and would like to continue.

_____

Signature   Date

I give permission for my interview to be audio taped ____ (please check to grant consent).

This informed consent statement has been approved by the University of Illinois.

Participants of this study will be given a copy of the consent form.

Bibliography

Abdullahi, Ishmail. 2007. Diversity and intercultural issues in library and information science (LIS) education." *New Library World* 108 (9/10): 453–459.

Adcock, Matthew, et al. n.d. Report of the Diversity Task Force: University Libraries. http://dante.uark.edu/Webdocs/committees/diversitytaskforce/DiversityPlan.pdf (accessed May 5, 2009).

Adkins, Denice, and Isabel Espinal. 2004. The diversity mandate *Library Journal* 129 (7): 52–54.

Alire, Camila. A. 1997. Ethnic populations: A model for statewide service. *American Libraries* 28 (10): 38–41.

Alire, Camila A., and Orlando Archibeque. 1998. *Serving Latino communities: A how-to-do-it manual for librarians.* New York: Neal-Schuman.

American Library Association. 1999. *Academic and public libraries: Data by race, ethnicity, and sex.* Chicago: American Library Association.

———. 2007a. *ALA policy manual.* Chicago: American Library Association.

———. 2007b. *Diversity counts.* Chicago: American Library Association.

———. 2008. Office for diversity website, www.ala.org/ala/aboutala/offices/diversity/index.cfm (accessed Jan. 7, 2009).

Anderson, James A. 1993. *Handbook for the assessment of diversity.* Raleigh, NC: North Carolina State University.

Arai, Marguerite, Maryanne Wanca-Thibault, and Pamela Shockley-Zalabak. 2001. Communication theory and training approaches for multiculturally diverse organizations: Have academics and practitioners missed the connection? *Public Personnel Management* 30 (4): 445–455.

Arzu, Anna N. 1995. Multicultural approach for curriculum development in the library and information sciences: Where are we going? *Public and Access Services Quarterly* 1 (3): 101–104.

Association for Library and Information Science Education. 2007. *Directory of LIS programs and faculty in the United States and Canada.* Chicago: Association for Library and Information Science Education.

Banks, James A. 2001. *Cultural diversity and education: Foundations, curriculum, and teaching,* 4th ed. Boston: Allyn & Bacon.

Bendick, Marc, Mary Lou Egan, and Suzanne. M. Lofhjelm. 2001. Workforce diversity training: From anti-discrimination compliance to organizational development. *Human Resource Planning* 2 (2): 10–25.

Black, Susan. 2002. What gets measured gets done: Using metrics to support diversity. *Canadian HR Reporter* 15 (22): 13–14.

Brewer, Julie. 2001. Reflections of an academic library residency program coordinator. In Raquel V. Cogell and Cindy A. Gruwell, eds. *Diversity in Libraries: Academic Residency Programs.* Westport, CT: Greenwood Press: 7–16.

Brown, Elinor. 2006. Knowing, valuing and shaping one's culture: A precursor to acknowledging, accepting and respecting the cultures of others. *Multicultural Education* 14 (1): 15–19.

Cameron, Kim S., and Robert E. Quinn. 1999. An introduction to changing organizational culture. In *Diagnosing and Changing Organizational Culture: Based on the Competing Values Framework,* 1–12. Upper Saddle River, NJ: Prentice Hall. http://webuser.bus.umich.edu/cameronk/CULTURE%20BOOK-CHAPTER%201.pdf (accessed Jan. 7, 2009).

Cardelle-Elawar, Maria, and Ann Nevin. 2003. The role of motivation on strengthening teacher identity: Emerging themes. *Action in Teacher Education* 25 (3): 48–58.

Chu, Clara M. 2002. Ethnic diversity in library and information science. *Library Quarterly* 72 (1): 136–138.

Colorado Department of Education. 2008a. Library diversity plans. www.cde.state.co.us/cdelib/diversity/Resources-Plan.htm (accessed Nov. 15, 2009).

———. 2008b. Library services to diverse and special populations. http://www.cde.state.co.us/cdelib/librarydiversity.htm (accessed Nov. 15, 2009).

Cross, Terry L., et al. 1989. *Towards a culturally competent system of care: A monograph on effective services for minority children who are severely emotionally disturbed.* Washington, DC: CASSP Technical Assistance Center, Georgetown University Child Development Center.

Daugherty, Martha, Jenny Logan, Matthew Turner, and David Compton. 2003. Associations among preservice teachers' psychological traits and classroom performance ratings. *The Teacher Educator* 38 (3): 151–168.

Day, Nancy E., and Betty J. Glick. 2000. Teaching diversity: A study of organizational needs and diversity curriculum in higher education. *Journal of Management Education* 24 (3): 338.

Decision Demographics. 2004. *Tabulations of the 1990 and 2000 census Public Use Microdata Sample (PUMS) files.* Arlington, VA: Decision Demographics.

Dewey, Barbara I., and Loretta Parham, eds. 2006. *Achieving diversity: A how-to-do-it manual for librarians.* New York: Neal-Schuman.

Dilevko, Juris, and Lisa Gottlieb. 2004. Working at tribal college and university libraries: A portrait. *Library & Information Science Research* 26 (1): 44–72.

East, Dennis, and R. Errol Lam. 1995. In search of multiculturalism in the library science curriculum. *Journal of Education for Library and Information Science* 36 (3): 199–216.

Elturk, Ghada. 2003. Diversity and cultural competency. *Colorado Libraries* 29 (4): 5–7. http://vnweb.hwwilsonweb.com/hww/jumpstart.jht ml?recid=0bc05f7a67b1790e183771395b86e5aac9cb21c842ce7ca4ff 96549abb34fa7c5728181d209d8c22&fmt=P (accessed Jan. 7, 2009).

Flowers, Lamont A. 2003. National study of diversity requirements in student affairs graduate programs. *NASPA Journal* 40 (4): 72–82.

Freiband, Susan. J. 1992. Multicultural issues and concerns in library education. *Journal of Education for Library and Information Science,* 33 (4): 287–294.

Gandhi, Smiti. 2000. Cultural diversity and libraries: Reaching the goal. *Current Studies in Librarianship* 24 (1/2): 55–65.

Glaviano, Cliff, and R. Errol Lam. 1990. Academic libraries and affirmative action: Approaching cultural diversity in the 1990's. *College and Research Libraries* 51 (6): 513–523.

Gollop, Claudia J. 1999. Library and information science education: Preparing librarians for a multicultural society. *College & Research Libraries* 60 (4): 385–395. www.ala.org/ala/mgrps/divs/acrl/publica-tions/crljournal/1999/jul/gollop.pdf (accessed Nov. 15, 2009).

Gomez, Martin J. 2000. Who is most qualified to serve our ethnic-minority communities? *American Libraries* 31 (11): 39–41.

Gupta, Kavita. 1999. *A practical guide to needs assessment.* San Francisco: Jossey-Bass/Pfeiffer.

Haro, Robert P. 1981. *Developing library and information services for Americans of Hispanic origin.* Metuchen, NJ: Scarecrow Press.

Healy, Charles. 1997. An operational definition of mentoring. In *Diversity in Higher Education: Mentoring and Diversity in Higher Education* (vol. 1), ed. Henry T. Frierson, Jr., 9–22. Greenwich, CT: JAI Press.

Hersey, Paul, Kenneth H. Blanchard, and Dewey E. Johnson. 2001. *Management of organization behavior: Leading human resources,* 8th ed. Upper Saddle River, NJ: Prentice Hall.

Holladay, Courtney L., Jennifer Knight, Danielle L. Paige, and Miguel Quiñones. 2003. The influence of organizational framing on attitudes toward diversity training. *Human Resource Development Quarterly* 14 (3): 245–263.

Horenstein, Bonnie. 1993. Job satisfaction of academic librarians: An examination of the relationships between satisfaction, faculty status, and participation. *College and Research Libraries* 54 (3): 255–269.

Houston Area Library System. 2004. Diversity: Customer service module 2. *Customer Service Training for Public Libraries.* www.hals.lib.tx.us/cust123/2intro.htm (accessed Nov. 15, 2009).

Howland, Joan S. 2001. Challenges of working in a multicultural environment. *Journal of Library Administration* 33 (1–2): 105–123.

Hubbard, Edward E. 2003. Assessing, measuring, and analyzing the impact of diversity initiatives. In *Handbook of Diversity Management: Beyond Awareness to Competency Based Learning,* ed. Deborah L. Plummer, 271–305. Lanham, MD: University Press of America.

Jameison, David, and Julie O'Mara. 1991. *Managing workforce 2000: Gaining the diversity advantage.* San Francisco: Jossey-Bass.

Joplin, Janice R. W., and Catherine S. Daus. 1997. Challenges of leading a diverse workforce. *Academy of Management Executive* 11 (3): 32–47.

Josey, E. J. 1993. The challenges of cultural diversity in the recruitment of faculty and students from diverse backgrounds. *Journal of Education for Library and Information Science* 34 (4): 302–311.

Josey, E. J., and Ismael Abdullahi. 2002. Why diversity in American libraries. *Library Management* 23 (1/2): 10–16.

Kaarst-Brown, Michelle L., Scott Nicholson, Gisela M. von Dran, and Jeffrey M. Stanton. 2004. Organizational cultures of libraries as a strategic resource. *Library Trends* 53 (1): 33–53.

Kaufman, Paula T. 2002. Where do the next "we" come from? Recruiting, retaining and developing our successors. *ARL Bimonthly Report* 221:1–5.

Kim, Kyung-Sun, and Joanna Sin Sei-Ching. 2008. Increasing ethnic diversity in LIS: Strategies suggested by librarians of color. *The Library Quarterly* 78 (2): 153–177.

Landry, Marie B. 2000. The effects of life satisfaction and job satisfaction on reference librarians and their work. *Reference and User Services Quarterly* 40 (2): 166–177.

Lanier, Patricia, Paula Phillips Carson, Kerry David Carson, & Joyce S. Phillips. 1997. What keeps academic librarians in the books? *The Journal of Academic Librarianship* 23 (3): 191–197.

Lester, Scott W., and Jill Kickul. 2001. Psychological contracts in the 21st century: What employees value most and how well organisations are responding to these expectations. *Human Resource Planning* 24 (1): 10–21.

Lillard, Linda L., and Barbara A. Wales. 2003. Strengthening the profession: Education and practitioner collaboration. *The Journal of Academic Librarianship* 29 (9): 316–319.

Love, Johnnieque B. 2001. The assessment of diversity initiatives in academic libraries. Co-published simultaneously in *Journal of Library Administration* (Haworth Information Press, an imprint of The Haworth Press, Inc.) 33 (1/2): 73–103.

Martin, Rebecca R. 1994. Changing the university climate: Three libraries respond to multicultural students. *Journal of Academic Librarianship* 20 (1): 2–9.

Mestre, Lori, et al. 1997. *Diversity and Multiculturalism Working Group Report.* Amherst, MA: University Library System, University of Massachusetts Amherst. http://web.archive.org/web/20070107063723/ http://www.library.umass.edu/plan/dmwg.htm (accessed Nov. 15, 2009).

Nance-Mitchell, Veronica. E. 1996. A multicultural library: Strategies for the twenty-first century. *College & Research Libraries* 57(5): 405–413. http://vnweb.hwwilsonweb.com/hww/jumpstart.jhtml?recid=0bc05 f7a67b1790e183771395b86e5aa3b826244e2157c525732bcd6470e fa25c9b5fb326f60644f&fmt=C (accessed Jan. 7, 2009).

Nandy, Subodh. 1985. Job satisfaction of the library professionals. *Herald of Library Science* 24 (Oct.): 295–300.

National Center for Cultural Competence. 2008. Cultural competence: Definition and conceptual framework. Georgetown University. www11.georgetown.edu/research/gucchd/nccc/foundations/frameworks.html (accessed Dec. 17, 2008).

Neely, Teresa Y., and Kuang-Hwei Lee-Smeltzer, eds. 2002. *Diversity now: People, collections, and services in academic libraries: Selected papers from the Big 12 Plus Libraries Consortium diversity conference.* Philadelphia: Haworth Press.

Ocean County Library. 2007. Diversity exchange: A database for library diversity programs. http://theoceancountylibrary.org/About/Diversity-Plan.htm (accessed Dec. 21, 2008).

Ohio Educator Standards Board. 2005. Educator standards board adopts revised definition of "cultural competency." *Educator Standards Board Monthly Online Update* (Nov. 1). http://esb.ode.state.oh.us/Communications/online_update_nov_05.aspx (accessed Jan. 7, 2009).

Peterson, Lorna. 1995. Strategies for infusing multicultural education into the library science curriculum. In *Culture Keepers II: Unity through Diversity, Proceedings of the Second National Conference of African American Librarians,* ed. Stanton Biddle, 73–76. Newark, NJ: Black Caucus of the ALA.

———. Curriculum reform and diversity. 2005. In *Unfinished Business: Race, Equity, and Diversity in Library and Information Science Education,* ed. Maurice B. Wheeler, 163–169. Lanham, MD: Scarecrow.

Potter, Lawrence, et al. 2006. *Diversity and multiculturalism action plan: Leading, practicing, and succeeding by example in a changing world.* Kalamazoo, MI: Western Michigan University. www.wmich.edu/diversityandinclusion/documents/Approved%20DMAP%204-19-06.pdf (accessed Dec. 17, 2008).

Press, Nancy Ottman, and Mary Diggs-Hobson. 2005. Providing health information to community members where they are: Characteristics of the culturally competent librarian. *Library Trends* 53 (3): 397–410.

Pressley, Michael, and Alysia D. Roehrig. 2004. Educational psychology in the modern era: 1960 to the present. In *Educational Psychology: A Century of Contributions,* ed. Barry J. Zimmerman and Dale H. Schunk, 333–366. Mahwah, NJ: Erlbaum.

Raju, Jayarani. 2003. The "core" in library and/or information science education and training. *Education for Information* 2 (4): 229–242.

Roy, Loriene. 2001. Diversity in the classroom: Incorporating service-learning experiences in the library and information science curriculum. *Journal of Education for Library and Information Science* 33 (4): 213–228.

Royse, Molly, Tiffany Conner, and Tamara Miller. 2006. Charting a course for diversity: An experience in climate assessment. *portal: Libraries and the Academy* 6 (1): 23–45.

Ruan, Lian, and Jian Anna Xiong. 2008. Career choices and advancement: Chinese American librarians in the 21st century. *Chinese Librarianship: An International Electronic Journal* 25. www.iclc.us/cliej/cl25RX2.htm (accessed Jan. 7, 2009).

Saye, Jerry D., and Katherine M. Wisser. 2003. Students. *ALISE Library and Information Science Statistical Report,* Table 11-4-A. Chicago: Association for Library and Information Science Education. http://ils.unc.edu/ALISE/2003/Students/Students01.htm (Jan. 7, 2009).

Schein, Edgar. 2004. *Organizational culture and leadership*, 3rd ed. San Francisco: Jossey-Bass.

Seidman, Irv. 2006. *Interviewing as qualitative research: A guide for researchers in education and the social sciences,* 3rd ed. New York: Teachers College Press.

Sierpe, Eino. 1999. Job satisfaction among librarians in English-language universities in Quebec. *Library and Information Science Research* 21 (4): 479–499.

Somerville, Mary M., and Gordon Yusko. 2008. The Librarians for Tomorrow project: Preparing San Jose's new generation of librarians for cultural communities. *Multicultural Review* 17 (2): 34–38.

Squire, Jan S. 1991. Job satisfaction and the ethnic minority librarian. *Library Administration & Management* 5 (Fall): 194–203.

Talbot, Donna M. 1996. Master's students' perspectives on their graduate education regarding issues of diversity. *NASPA Journal* 33 (3): 163–178.

Talbot, Donna M., and Cathering Kocarek. 1997. Student affairs graduate faculty members' knowledge, comfort, and behaviors regarding issues of diversity. *Journal of College Student Development* 38 (30): 278–287.

Thomas, R. Roosevelt. 1990. From affirmative action to affirming diversity. *Harvard Business Review* 68:107–117.

Thornton, Joyce K. 2000. Job satisfaction of librarians of African descent employed in ARL academic libraries. *College & Research Libraries* 61 (3): 217–232.

———. 2001. African American female librarians: A study of job satisfaction. *Journal of Library Administration* 33 (1/2): 141–164.

United States Bureau of the Census. 2009. *Statistical abstract of the United States.* Washington, DC: U.S. Census Bureau.www.census.gov/compendia/statab/cats/population.html (accessed Jan. 7, 2009).

———. 2008 (Aug. 14). Projections of the population by sex, race, and Hispanic origin for the United States: 2010 to 2050. Washington, DC: U.S. Census Bureau, Population Division, Table 4 (NP2008-T4). www.census.gov/population/www/projections/summarytables.html (accessed Jan. 7, 2009).

———. 2000. American community survey. Washington, DC: U.S. Census Bureau. www.census.gov/acs/www/SBasics/SQuest/SQuest1.htm (accessed Jan. 7, 2009).

University of Massachusetts Amherst Libraries. 2005 (Jan. 19). UMass Amherst Libraries'community, diversity, and social justice action plan. www.library.umass.edu/assets/aboutus/attachments/CDSJActionPlanReport.pdf (accessed Nov. 9, 2009).

Vaughan, William J., and J. D. *Dunn. 1974.* A study of job satisfaction in six university libraries, *College and Research Libraries* 35: 163–177. Web Junction. 2008. Populations served. www.webjunction.org/populations-served (accessed Jan. 7, 2009).

Wheeler, Maurice B. 2005. Faculty development and cultural diversity in teaching: LIS education's last frontier. In *Unfinished Business: Race, Equity, and Diversity in Library and Information Science Education,* ed. Maurice B. Wheeler, 181–194. Lanham, MD: Scarecrow.

Williams, James F., II. 1999. Managing diversity: Library management in light of the dismantling of affirmative action. *Journal of Library Administration* 27 (1–2): 45.

Winston, Mark D., ed. 1999. *Managing multiculturalism and diversity in the library.* Philadelphia: Haworth Press.

Zeilchner, Kenneth, and Kristin Hoeft. 1996. Teacher socialization for cultural diversity. In *Handbook of Research on Teacher Education Handbook,* 2nd ed., ed. John Sikula, Thomas J. Buttery, and Edith Guyton, 525–547. New York: Macmillan.

Index